THE WHO'S BUYING SERIES
BY THE NEW STRATEGIST EDITORS

Who's Buying

Alcoholic
and
Nonalcoholic
Beverages

3rd EDITION

New Strategist Publications, Inc.
P.O. Box 242, Ithaca, New York 14851
800/848-0842; 607/273-0913
www.newstrategist.com

ISBN 978-1-933588-11-7

Printed in the United States of America

Contents

About the data in "Who's Buying Alcoholic and Nonalcoholic Beverages"

Introduction

The spending data in *Who's Buying Alcoholic and Nonalcoholic Beverages* are based on the Bureau of Labor Statistics' Consumer Expenditure Survey, an ongoing, nationwide survey of household spending. The Consumer Expenditure Survey is a complete accounting of household expenditures, including everything from big-ticket items such as homes and cars, to small purchases like laundry detergent and videos. The survey does not include expenditures by government, business, or institutions. The lag time between data collection and dissemination is about two years. The data in this report are from the 2004 Consumer Expenditure Survey, unless otherwise noted.

To produce this report, New Strategist Publications analyzed the Consumer Expenditure Survey's average household spending data in a variety of ways, calculating household spending indexes, aggregate (or total) household spending, and market shares. Spending data by age, household income, household type, race, Hispanic origin, region of residence, and education are shown in this report. These analyses are presented in two formats—for all product categories by demographic characteristic and for all demographic characteristics by product category.

Definition of consumer unit

The Consumer Expenditure Survey uses consumer unit rather than household as the sampling unit. The term "household" is used interchangeably with the term "consumer unit" in this report for convenience, although they are not exactly the same. Some households contain more than one consumer unit.

The Bureau of Labor Statistics defines consumer unit as either: (1) members of a household who are related by blood, marriage, adoption, or other legal arrangements; (2) a person living alone or sharing a household with others or living as a roomer in a private home or lodging house or in permanent living quarters in a hotel or motel, but who is financially independent; or (3) two or more persons living together who pool their income to make joint expenditure decisions. The bureau defines financial independence in terms of "the three major expenses categories: housing, food, and other living expenses. To be considered financially independent, at least two of the three major expense categories have to be provided by the respondent."

The Census Bureau uses household as its sampling unit in the decennial census and in the monthly Current Population Survey. The Census Bureau's household "consists of all persons who occupy a housing unit. A house, an apartment or other groups of rooms, or a single room is regarded as a housing unit when it is occupied or intended for occupancy as separate living quarters; that is, when the occupants do not live and eat with any other persons in the structure and there is direct access from the outside or through a common hall." The definition goes on to specify that "a household includes the related family members and all the unrelated persons, if any, such as lodgers, foster children, wards, or employees who share the housing unit. A person living alone in a housing unit or a group of unrelated persons sharing a housing unit as partners is also counted as a household. The count of households excludes group quarters."

Because there can be more than one consumer unit in a household, consumer units outnumber households by several million. Young adults under age 25 head most of the additional consumer units.

How to use the tables in this report

The starting point for all calculations are the unpublished, detailed average household spending data collected by the Consumer Expenditure Survey. These numbers are shown on the report's average spending tables and on each of the product-specific tables. New Strategist's editors calculated the other figures in the report based on the average figures. The indexed spending tables and the indexed spending column (Best Customers) on the product-specific tables reveal whether spending by households in a given segment is above or below the average for all households and by how much. The total (or aggregate) spending tables show the overall size of the market. The market share tables and market share column (Biggest Customers) on the product-specific tables reveal how much spending each household segment controls. These analyses are described in detail below.

• **Average Spending** The average spending figures show the average annual spending of households on alcoholic and nonalcoholic beverages in 2004. The Consumer Expenditure Survey produces average spending data for all households in a segment, e.g., all households with a householder aged 25 to 34, not just those purchasing an item. When examining spending data, it is important to remember that by including both purchasers and nonpurchasers in the calculation, the average is less than the amount spent on the item by buyers. (See the Table 1 for the percentage of households spending on alcoholic and nonalcoholic beverages in 2004 and how much the purchasers spent.)

Because average spending figures include both buyers and nonbuyers, they reveal spending patterns by demographic characteristic. By knowing who is most likely to spend on an item, marketers can target their advertising and promotions more efficiently, and businesses can determine the market potential of a product or service in a city or neighborhood. By multiplying the average amount households spend on wine or beer by the number of households in an area, for example, a shop owner can estimate the potential size of the local market for alcoholic beverages.

• **Indexed Spending (Best Customers)** The indexed spending figures compare the spending of each household segment with that of the average household. To compute the indexes, New Strategist divides the average amount each household segment spends on an item by average household spending and multiplies the resulting figure by 100.

An index of 100 is the average for all households. An index of 125 means the spending of a household segment is 25 percent above average (100 plus 25). An index of 75 indicates spending that is 25 percent below the average for all households (100 minus 25). Indexed spending figures identify the best customers for a product or service. Households with an index of 178 for wine, for example, are a strong market for this product. Those with an index below 100 are either a weak or an underserved market.

Spending indexes can reveal hidden markets—household segments with a high propensity to buy a particular product or service but which are overshadowed by household segments that account for a larger share of the market. Householders aged 55 to 64, for example, account for 19 percent of the market for alcoholic beverages purchased on trips versus the larger 21 percent share accounted for by householders aged 35 to 44. But a look at the indexed spending figures reveals that, in fact, older householders are the better customers, spending 28 percent more than the average household on alcohol while traveling compared with an average index of 101 for the younger age group. Resorts can use this information to target the customers most likely to spend on alcoholic beverages while traveling.

Note that because of sampling errors, small differences in index values may not be significant. But the broader patterns revealed by indexes can guide marketers to the best customers.

• **Total (Aggregate) Spending** To produce the total (aggregate) spending figures, New Strategist multiplies average spending by the number of households in a segment. The result is the dollar size of the total household market and of each market segment. All totals are shown in thousands of dollars. To convert the numbers in the total spending tables to dollars, you must append "000" to the number. For example, households headed by people aged 45 to 54 spent approximately $1.3 billion on coffee in 2004 ($820,435,000 on roasted coffee and $510,994,000 on instant and freeze-dried coffee).

When comparing the total spending figures in this report with total spending estimates from the Bureau of Economic Analysis, other government agencies, or trade associations, keep in mind that the Consumer Expenditure Survey includes only household spending, not spending by businesses or institutions. Sales data also will differ from household spending totals because sales figures for consumer products include the value of goods sold to industries, government, and foreign markets, which can be a significant proportion of sales.

• **Market Shares (Biggest Customers)** New Strategist produces market share figures by converting total (aggregate) spending data into percentages. To calculate the percentage of total spending on an item that is controlled by a demographic segment—i.e., its market share—the segment's total spending on the item is divided by aggregate household spending on the item.

Market shares reveal the biggest customers—the demographic segments that account for the largest share of spending on a particular product or service. In 2004, for example, households headed by college graduates accounted for 57 percent of spending on wine consumed at home, a much greater percentage than their 28 percent share of consumer units. By targeting only the best-educated consumers, wine marketers can reach the majority of their customers. There is a danger here, however. By single-mindedly targeting the biggest customers, businesses cannot nurture potential growth markets. With competition for customers more heated than ever, targeting potential markets is increasingly important to business survival.

• **Product-Specific Tables** The product-specific tables reveal at a glance the demographic characteristics of spending by individual product category. These tables show average spending, indexed spending (Best Customers), and market shares (Biggest Customers) by age, income, household type, race and Hispanic origin, region of residence, and education. If you want to see the spending pattern for an individual product at a glance, these are the tables for you.

History and methodology of the Consumer Expenditure Survey

The Consumer Expenditure Survey is an ongoing study of the day-to-day spending of American households. In taking the survey, government interviewers collect spending data on products and services as well as the amount and sources of household income, changes in savings and debt, and demographic and economic characteristics of household members. The Bureau of the Census collects data for the CEX under contract with the Bureau of Labor Statistics, which is responsible for analysis and release of the survey data.

Since the late nineteenth century, the federal government has conducted expenditure surveys about every ten years. Although the results have been used for a variety of purposes, their primary application is to track consumer prices. In 1980 the CEX became a continuous survey with annual release of data (with a lag time of about two years between data collection and release). The survey is used to update prices for the market basket of products and services used in calculating the Consumer Price Index.

The CEX consists of two separate surveys: an interview survey and a diary survey. In the interview portion of the survey, respondents are asked each quarter for five consecutive quarters to report their expenditures for the previous three months. The purchase of big-ticket items such as houses, cars, and major appliances, or recurring expenses such as insurance premiums, utility payments, and rent are recorded by the interview survey. The interview component covers about 95 percent of all expenditures.

Expenditures on small, frequently purchased items are recorded during a two-week period by the diary survey. These detailed records include expenses for food and beverages purchased in grocery stores and at restaurants, as well as other items such as tobacco, housekeeping supplies, nonprescription drugs, and personal care products and services. The diary survey is intended to capture expenditures respondents are likely to forget or recall incorrectly over longer periods of time.

Two separate, nationally representative samples are used for the interview and diary surveys. For the interview survey, about 7,500 consumer units are interviewed on a rotating panel basis each quarter for five consecutive quarters. Another 7,500 consumer units keep weekly diaries of spending for two consecutive weeks. Data collection is carried out in 105 areas of the country.

The Bureau of Labor Statistics reviews, audits, and cleans the data, and then weights them to reflect the number and characteristics of all U.S. consumer units. Like any sample survey, the CEX is subject to two major types of error. Nonsampling error occurs when respondents misinterpret questions or interviewers are inconsistent in the way they ask questions or record answers. Respondents may forget items, recall expenses incorrectly, or deliberately give wrong answers. A respondent may remember how much he or she spent at the grocery store but forget the items picked up at a local convenience store. Nonsampling error can also be caused by mistakes during the various stages of data processing and refinement.

Sampling error occurs when a sample does not accurately represent the population it is supposed to represent. This kind of error is present in every sample-based survey and is minimized by using a proper sampling procedure. Standard error tables documenting the extent of sampling error in the CEX are available from the Bureau of Labor Statistics at http://www.bls.gov/cex/csxstnderror.htm.

Although the CEX is the best source of information about the spending behavior of American households, it should be treated with caution because of the above problems.

For more information

To find out more about the CEX, contact the specialists at the Bureau of Labor Statistics at (202) 691-6900, or visit the Consumer Expenditure Survey home page at http://www.bls.gov/cex/. The web site includes news releases, technical documentation, and current and historical summary-level CEX data. The detailed average spending data shown in this report are available from the Bureau of Labor Statistics only by special request.

For a comprehensive look at detailed household spending data for all products and services, see the 11th edition of *Household Spending: Who Spends How Much on What*. To see the best and biggest customers for the complete array of products and services examined by the CEX, see the fourth edition of *Best Customers: Demographics of Consumer Demand*. To download spending reports for individual product and service categories, visit nSpend, the instant-answer service, at http://www.nspend.com.

New Strategist's books are available in hardcopy or as downloads by visiting http://www.newstrategist.com or by calling 1-800-848-0842.

Table 1. Percent Reporting Expenditure and Amount Spent, Average Week or Quarter 2004

(percent of consumer units reporting expenditure and amount spent by purchasers during an average week or quarter, 2004)

	average week	
	percent reporting expenditure	amount spent by purchasers
ALCOHOLIC BEVERAGES	**28.3%**	**$28.58**
Consumed at home	**19.6**	**27.24**
Beer and ale	13.5	18.77
Whiskey	1.5	27.45
Wine	7.1	25.53
Other alcoholic beverages	2.8	20.64
Consumed away from home (except on trips)	**14.9**	**18.49**
Beer and ale at restaurants, bars, etc.	12.3	12.00
Wine at restaurants, bars, etc.	4.9	8.70
Other alcoholic beverages at restaurants, bars, etc.	5.7	15.17
NONALCOHOLIC BEVERAGES		
Carbonated drinks, colas	35.2	5.12
Carbonated drinks, noncolas	26.2	3.51
Coffee	12.8	5.88
Roasted coffee	11.5	4.09
Instant and freeze-dried coffee	9.6	2.93
Frozen fruit juices, except orange	1.9	2.12
Frozen orange juice	3.0	2.70
Fruit juice, canned and bottled	26.3	4.03
Fruit juice, fresh	11.1	3.79
Fruit-flavored drinks	11.2	3.41
Milk, fresh	54.7	4.53
Other nonalcoholic beverages and ice	23.7	5.69
Tea	8.9	3.83
Vegetable juice	6.1	2.80

	average quarter	
	percent reporting expenditure	amount spent by purchasers
Alcoholic beverages purchased on trips	**12.1%**	**$79.28**

Source: Calculations by New Strategist based on the 2004 Consumer Expenditure Survey

Household Spending Trends: 2000 to 2004

Between 2000 and 2004, spending by the average household rose 4 percent, to $43,395, after adjusting for inflation. At the same time, average household income grew by a larger 11 percent. The considerable gap between income growth and spending growth reveals consumer caution, despite the improving economy. The pundits might accuse Americans of spending beyond their means, but in fact the steady rise in consumer spending at the national level primarily is the result of demographic change—population growth and the aging of the baby-boom generation into the peak earning and spending years.

Much of the growth in household spending between 2000 and 2004 was involuntary, brought about by the ever-larger claim of necessities on the household budget. After adjusting for inflation, the average household spent 11 percent more on property taxes in 2004 than in 2000. Spending on gasoline rose 13 percent during those years. Spending on vehicle insurance also grew 13 percent. Out-of-pocket spending on health insurance increased by an enormous 24 percent. Spending on education rose an even greater 31 percent.

Declines in discretionary spending are evident in the 2000 to 2004 trends. Spending on "other lodging," a category that includes hotel and motel expenses, fell 10 percent, after adjusting for inflation. Spending on furniture declined 3 percent, women's apparel fell 5 percent, and shoes lost an even larger 13 percent. Spending on public transportation (a category dominated by airline fares) declined 6 percent. Households cut their spending on fees and admissions to entertainment events by 7 percent and reading material by 19 percent.

Contrary to popular perception, Americans are cautious spenders at the individual household level. The recession of 2001 followed by the lackluster recovery forced households to spend less on many discretionary items to make ends meet. Rapidly rising energy costs are now reducing discretionary spending even further. With the aging baby-boom generation entering its sixties and leaving the peak spending years behind, average household spending is not likely to grow much in the years ahead. American businesses will have to adapt to a new economic landscape, one in which affluence is becoming less common and the middle class is struggling to stay afloat. The globalization of the workforce coupled with rising energy prices and an increasingly troubled health insurance system will make our future very different from our past.

Table 2. Household Spending Trends, 2000 to 2004

(average annual spending of total consumer units, 2000 and 2004; percent change, 2000–04; in 2004 dollars)

	2004	2000	percent change 2000–04
Number of consumer units (in 000s)	116,282	109,367	6.3%
Average before-tax income	$54,453	$48,975	11.2
Average annual spending	**43,395**	**41,731**	**4.0**
FOOD	**5,781**	**5,658**	**2.2**
Food at home	**3,347**	**3,314**	**1.0**
Cereals and bakery products	461	497	–7.2
Cereals and cereal products	154	171	–10.0
Bakery products	307	326	–5.8
Meats, poultry, fish, and eggs	880	872	0.9
Beef	265	261	1.5
Pork	181	183	–1.2
Other meats	108	111	–2.5
Poultry	156	159	–1.9
Fish and seafood	128	121	6.1
Eggs	42	37	12.6
Dairy products	371	356	4.1
Fresh milk and cream	144	144	0.2
Other dairy products	226	212	6.8
Fruits and vegetables	561	571	–1.8
Fresh fruits	187	179	4.6
Fresh vegetables	183	174	4.9
Processed fruits	110	126	–12.8
Processed vegetables	82	92	–11.0
Other food at home	1,075	1,017	5.7
Sugar and other sweets	128	128	–0.3
Fats and oils	89	91	–2.2
Miscellaneous foods	527	479	9.9
Nonalcoholic beverages	290	274	5.8
Food prepared by consumer unit on trips	41	44	–6.6
Food away from home	**2,434**	**2,344**	**3.8**
ALCOHOLIC BEVERAGES	**459**	**408**	**12.5**
HOUSING	**13,918**	**13,513**	**3.0**
Shelter	**7,998**	**7,803**	**2.5**
Owned dwellings	5,324	5,048	5.5
Mortgage interest and charges	2,936	2,895	1.4
Property taxes	1,391	1,249	11.3
Maintenance, repair, insurance, other expenses	997	905	10.2
Rented dwellings	2,201	2,231	–1.3
Other lodging	473	524	–9.8
Utilities, fuels, and public services	**2,927**	**2,730**	**7.2**
Natural gas	424	337	25.9
Electricity	1,064	999	6.5

	2004	2000	percent change 2000–04
Fuel oil and other fuels	$121	$106	13.7%
Telephone	990	962	2.9
Water and other public services	327	325	0.7
Household services	**753**	**750**	**0.4**
Personal services	300	358	–16.1
Other household services	453	393	15.4
Housekeeping supplies	**594**	**529**	**12.4**
Laundry and cleaning supplies	149	144	3.7
Other household products	290	248	17.0
Postage and stationery	155	138	12.1
Household furnishings and equipment	**1,646**	**1,699**	**–3.1**
Household textiles	158	116	35.9
Furniture	417	429	–2.8
Floor coverings	52	48	7.7
Major appliances	204	207	–1.6
Small appliances, miscellaneous housewares	105	95	10.0
Miscellaneous household equipment	711	802	–11.3
APPAREL AND RELATED SERVICES	**1,816**	**2,036**	**–10.8**
Men and boys	**406**	**483**	**–15.9**
Men, aged 16 or older	317	377	–16.0
Boys, aged 2 to 15	89	105	–15.5
Women and girls	**739**	**795**	**–7.1**
Women, aged 16 or older	631	666	–5.2
Girls, aged 2 to 15	108	129	–16.6
Children under age 2	**79**	**90**	**–12.2**
Footwear	**329**	**376**	**–12.6**
Other apparel products and services	**264**	**292**	**–9.5**
TRANSPORTATION	**7,801**	**8,136**	**–4.1**
Vehicle purchases	**3,397**	**3,749**	**–9.4**
Cars and trucks, new	1,748	1,761	–0.7
Cars and trucks, used	1,582	1,941	–18.5
Gasoline and motor oil	**1,598**	**1,416**	**12.8**
Other vehicle expenses	**2,365**	**2,502**	**–5.5**
Vehicle finance charges	323	360	–10.2
Maintenance and repairs	652	684	–4.7
Vehicle insurance	964	853	13.0
Vehicle rentals, leases, licenses, other charges	426	604	–29.5
Public transportation	**441**	**468**	**–5.8**
HEALTH CARE	**2,574**	**2,266**	**13.6**
Health insurance	1,332	1,078	23.5
Medical services	648	623	4.0
Drugs	480	456	5.2
Medical supplies	114	109	5.0
ENTERTAINMENT	**2,218**	**2,044**	**8.5**
Fees and admissions	528	565	–6.5
Television, radio, and sound equipment	788	682	15.5
Pets, toys, and playground equipment	381	366	4.0
Other entertainment products and services	522	431	21.1

	2004	2000	percent change 2000–04
PERSONAL CARE PRODUCTS AND SERVICES	$581	$619	−6.1%
READING	130	160	−18.8
EDUCATION	905	693	30.5
TOBACCO PRODUCTS AND SMOKING SUPPLIES	288	350	−17.7
MISCELLANEOUS	690	851	−18.9
CASH CONTRIBUTIONS	1,408	1,307	7.7
PERSONAL INSURANCE AND PENSIONS	4,823	3,691	30.7
Life and other personal insurance	390	438	−10.9
Pensions and Social Security	4,433	3,253	36.3
PERSONAL TAXES	2,166	3,419	−36.6
Federal income taxes	1,519	2,642	−42.5
State and local income taxes	472	616	−23.4
Other taxes	175	160	9.3
GIFTS FOR NONHOUSEHOLD MEMBERS	1,215	1,188	2.3

Note: Average spending is rounded to the nearest dollar. The percent change calculation is based on unrounded figures. The Bureau of Labor Statistics uses consumer unit rather than household as the sampling unit in the Consumer Expenditure Survey. For the definition of consumer unit, see the glossary. Spending on gifts is also included in the preceding product and service categories.

Source: Bureau of Labor Statistics, 2000 and 2004 Consumer Expenditure Surveys, Internet site http://www.bls.gov/cex/; calculations by New Strategist

Household Spending on Alcoholic Beverages, 2004

Between 2000 and 2004, spending on alcoholic beverages by the average household climbed 13 percent, after adjusting for inflation. Behind the increase was the aging of the baby-boom generation into the empty-nest years, when spending on alcohol increases. Beer spending rose 8 percent between 2000 and 2004, while spending on wine increased 9 percent. Spending on whiskey and other alcoholic beverages climbed by a substantial 35 percent during those years. Spending on alcoholic beverages purchased on trips increased only 2 percent between 2000 and 2004.

The average household spent $459 on alcoholic beverages in 2004. The figure may seem low because it is an average for all households, including both those who purchased alcoholic beverages and those who did not. The Bureau of Labor Statistics reports that during an average week of 2004, 28 percent of households purchased alcoholic beverages, spending $28.58 on them.

Most spending in the alcohol category is for beverages consumed at home. In 2004, 60 percent of alcoholic beverage spending was for home consumption and 40 percent for alcohol consumed at restaurants, bars, or on trips. Beer accounts for 45 percent of alcohol spending, wine for 25 percent, whiskey and other alcohol for 21 percent.

Spending by age

The biggest spenders on alcoholic beverages, householders aged 25 to 44, devote 14 to 16 percent more than the average household to the category. Spending on beer consumed at home declines with age, from a peak of 39 percent above average for householders under age 35 to below-average spending for householders aged 55 or older. In contrast, spending on wine consumed at home peaks in middle age, at 18 to 43 percent above average for householders aged 35 to 64. Householders aged 55 to 64 spend the most on alcoholic beverages purchased on trips (28 percent more than average). Householders under age 35 spend the most on alcohol at restaurants and bars.

Spending by household income

Not surprisingly, the most affluent households are also the ones that spend the most on alcoholic beverages. In 2004, households with incomes of $100,000 or more spent more than twice as much as the average household on alcoholic beverages. The most affluent households spend considerably more than those with lower incomes on all but one alcoholic beverage category: beer and ale consumed at home. Households with incomes of $100,000 or more are by far the best customers of wine and alcoholic beverages purchased on trips, spending nearly three times the average on these items.

Spending by household type

Married couples without children at home (most are empty-nesters) spend the most on alcoholic beverages—23 percent more than the average household. They are the biggest spenders on wine, whiskey, and other alcoholic beverages consumed at home and every type of alcoholic beverage consumed at restaurants and bars. They are also the best customers of alcoholic beverages purchased on trips (with an index of 156). Married couples with school-aged children are the biggest spenders on beer consumed at home.

Spending by race and Hispanic origin

Asian, black, and Hispanic households spend much less than the average household on alcoholic beverages. Blacks spend just 37 percent as much as the average household on alcoholic beverages, while Asians spend 71 percent of the average and Hispanics 70 percent. Hispanics spend 25 percent more than average on beer consumed at home.

Spending by region

Households in the South spend 24 percent less than the average household on alcoholic beverages. Their spending is below average for almost every type of alcoholic beverage. Households in the Northeast spend 36 percent more than average on alcoholic beverages. Households in the West spend 16 percent more than average on alcoholic beverages, with spending 30 percent above average for wine consumed at home. Households in the Midwest spend 7 percent less than average on alcoholic beverages.

Spending by education

Spending on alcoholic beverages rises with education, in part because educated householders have higher incomes. College graduates spend 55 percent more than the average household on alcoholic beverages and account for 43 percent of the market. They spend twice the average on wine consumed at home. High school graduates spend an average amount on beer consumed at home.

Table 3. Alcoholic Beverage Spending, 2000 to 2004

(average annual and percent distribution of household spending on alcoholic beverages, 2000 to 2004; percent change in spending, 2000–04; in 2004 dollars; ranked by amount spent)

	2004		2000		
	average household spending	percent distribution	average household spending (in 2004$)	percent distribution	percent change 2000–04
Average household spending on alcoholic beverages	**$459.27**	**100.0%**	**$407.87**	**100.0%**	**12.6%**
Beer and ale	207.63	45.2	191.39	46.9	8.5
Beer and ale at home	131.31	28.6	122.87	30.1	6.9
Beer and ale at restaurants, bars	76.32	16.6	68.52	16.8	11.4
Wine	116.84	25.4	107.32	26.3	8.9
Wine at home	94.55	20.6	87.80	21.5	7.7
Wine at restaurants, bars	22.29	4.9	19.52	4.8	14.2
Whiskey and other alcohol	96.44	21.0	71.60	17.6	34.7
Whiskey and other alcohol at home	51.73	11.3	37.94	9.3	36.3
Whiskey and other alcohol at restaurants, bars	44.71	9.7	33.66	8.3	32.8
Alcoholic beverages on trips	38.37	8.4	37.56	9.2	2.2

Source: Bureau of Labor Statistics, 2000 and 2004 Consumer Expenditure Surveys; calculations by New Strategist

Table 4. Alcoholic Beverages: Average spending by age, 2004

(average annual spending of consumer units (CU) on alcoholic beverages, by age of consumer unit reference person, 2004)

	total consumer units	under 25	25 to 34	35 to 44	45 to 54	55 to 64	65 to 74	75+
Number of consumer units (in 000s)	116,282	8,817	19,439	24,070	23,712	17,479	11,230	11,536
Number of persons per CU	2.5	1.9	2.9	3.2	2.7	2.1	1.9	1.5
Average before-tax income of CU	$54,453.00	$22,840.00	$52,484.00	$65,515.00	$70,434.00	$61,031.00	$42,137.00	$28,028.00
Average spending of CU, total	43,394.87	24,534.56	42,700.54	50,401.62	52,764.36	47,298.58	36,511.98	25,763.32
ALCOHOLIC BEVERAGES	459.27	502.53	521.87	534.72	501.52	456.55	329.36	190.13
Consumed at home	277.59	277.79	281.72	363.54	294.30	279.03	199.75	120.08
Beer and ale	131.31	182.80	182.57	172.98	132.46	93.87	55.45	37.72
Whiskey	21.66	24.54	11.95	26.93	21.55	26.69	23.09	15.94
Wine	94.55	38.62	59.49	135.56	111.59	115.32	92.66	45.09
Other alcoholic beverages	30.07	31.83	27.71	28.06	28.69	43.15	28.56	21.32
Consumed away from home	181.68	224.73	240.15	171.18	207.22	177.53	129.61	70.05
Beer and ale at restaurants, bars	76.32	102.53	106.75	68.69	88.64	69.58	49.59	28.45
Wine at restaurants, bars	22.29	32.57	29.61	19.29	25.68	20.67	15.80	9.28
Whiskey and other alcohol at restaurants, bars	44.71	62.90	63.87	44.28	48.82	38.24	26.82	15.83
Alcoholic beverages purchased on trips	38.37	26.73	39.93	38.92	44.08	49.04	37.40	16.49

Source: Bureau of Labor Statistics, unpublished tables from the 2004 Consumer Expenditure Survey

Table 5. Alcoholic Beverages: Indexed spending by age, 2004

(indexed average annual spending of consumer units (CU) on alcoholic beverages, by age of consumer unit reference person, 2004; index definition: an index of 100 is the average for all consumer units; an index of 132 means that spending by consumer units in that group is 32 percent above the average for all consumer units; an index of 68 indicates spending that is 32 percent below the average for all consumer units)

	total consumer units	under 25	25 to 34	35 to 44	45 to 54	55 to 64	65 to 74	75+
Average spending of CU, total	$43,395	$24,535	$42,701	$50,402	$52,764	$47,299	$36,512	$25,763
Average spending of CU, index	100	57	98	116	122	109	84	59
ALCOHOLIC BEVERAGES	100	109	114	116	109	99	72	41
Consumed at home	100	100	101	131	106	101	72	43
Beer and ale	100	139	139	132	101	71	42	29
Whiskey	100	113	55	124	99	123	107	74
Wine	100	41	63	143	118	122	98	48
Other alcoholic beverages	100	106	92	93	95	143	95	71
Consumed away from home	100	124	132	94	114	98	71	39
Beer and ale at restaurants, bars	100	134	140	90	116	91	65	37
Wine at restaurants, bars	100	146	133	87	115	93	71	42
Whiskey and other alcohol at restaurants, bars	100	141	143	99	109	86	60	35
Alcoholic beverages purchased on trips	100	70	104	101	115	128	97	43

Source: Calculations by New Strategist based on the Bureau of Labor Statistics 2004 Consumer Expenditure Survey

Table 6. Alcoholic Beverages: Total spending by age, 2004

(total annual spending on alcoholic beverages, by consumer unit (CU) age group, 2004; consumer units and dollars in thousands)

	total consumer units	under 25	25 to 34	35 to 44	45 to 54	55 to 64	65 to 74	75+
Number of consumer units	116,282	8,817	19,439	24,070	23,712	17,479	11,230	11,536
Total spending of all CUs	$5,046,042,273	$216,321,216	$830,055,797	$1,213,166,993	$1,251,148,504	$826,731,880	$410,029,535	$297,205,660
ALCOHOLIC BEVERAGES	53,404,834	4,430,807	10,144,631	12,870,710	11,892,042	7,980,037	3,698,713	2,193,340
Consumed at home	32,278,720	2,449,274	5,476,355	8,750,408	6,978,442	4,877,165	2,243,193	1,385,243
Beer and ale	15,268,989	1,611,748	3,548,978	4,163,629	3,140,892	1,640,754	622,704	435,138
Whiskey	2,518,668	216,369	232,296	648,205	510,994	466,515	259,301	183,884
Wine	10,994,463	340,513	1,156,426	3,262,929	2,646,022	2,015,678	1,040,572	520,158
Other alcoholic beverages	3,496,600	280,645	538,655	675,404	680,297	754,219	320,729	245,948
Consumed away from home	21,126,114	1,981,444	4,668,276	4,120,303	4,913,601	3,103,047	1,455,520	**808,097**
Beer and ale at restaurants, bars	8,874,642	904,007	2,075,113	1,653,368	2,101,832	1,216,189	556,896	328,199
Wine at restaurants, bars	2,591,926	287,170	575,589	464,310	608,924	361,291	177,434	107,054
Whiskey and other alcohol at restaurants, bars	5,198,968	554,589	1,241,569	1,065,820	1,157,620	668,397	301,189	182,615
Alcoholic beverages purchased on trips	4,461,740	235,678	776,199	936,804	1,045,225	857,170	420,002	190,229

Note: Numbers may not add to total because of rounding.
Source: Calculations by New Strategist based on the Bureau of Labor Statistics 2004 Consumer Expenditure Survey

Table 7. Alcoholic Beverages: Market shares by age, 2004

(percentage of total annual spending on alcoholic beverages accounted for by consumer unit age groups, 2004)

	total consumer units	under 25	25 to 34	35 to 44	45 to 54	55 to 64	65 to 74	75+
Share of total consumer units	100.0%	7.6%	16.7%	20.7%	20.4%	15.0%	9.7%	9.9%
Share of total before-tax income	100.0	3.2	16.1	24.9	26.4	16.8	7.5	5.1
Share of total spending	100.0	4.3	16.4	24.0	24.8	16.4	8.1	5.9
ALCOHOLIC BEVERAGES	100.0	8.3	19.0	24.1	22.3	14.9	6.9	4.1
Consumed at home	100.0	7.6	17.0	27.1	21.6	15.1	6.9	4.3
Beer and ale	100.0	10.6	23.2	27.3	20.6	10.7	4.1	2.8
Whiskey	100.0	8.6	9.2	25.7	20.3	18.5	10.3	7.3
Wine	100.0	3.1	10.5	29.7	24.1	18.3	9.5	4.7
Other alcoholic beverages	100.0	8.0	15.4	19.3	19.5	21.6	9.2	7.0
Consumed away from home	100.0	9.4	22.1	19.5	23.3	14.7	6.9	3.8
Beer and ale at restaurants, bars	100.0	10.2	23.4	18.6	23.7	13.7	6.3	3.7
Wine at restaurants, bars	100.0	11.1	22.2	17.9	23.5	13.9	6.8	4.1
Whiskey and other alcohol at restaurants, bars	100.0	10.7	23.9	20.5	22.3	12.9	5.8	3.5
Alcoholic beverages purchased on trips	100.0	5.3	17.4	21.0	23.4	19.2	9.4	4.3

Note: Numbers may not add to total because of rounding.
Source: Calculations by New Strategist based on the Bureau of Labor Statistics 2004 Consumer Expenditure Survey

Table 8. Alcoholic Beverages: Average spending by income, 2004

(average annual spending on alcoholic beverages, by before-tax income of consumer units (CU), 2004)

	total consumer units	under $20,000	$20,000–$39,999	$40,000–$49,999	$50,000–$69,999	$70,000–$79,999	$80,000–$99,999	$100,000 or more
Number of consumer units (in 000s)	116,282	28,898	27,297	11,374	18,069	6,461	9,246	14,937
Number of persons per CU	2.5	1.8	2.3	2.6	2.8	3.0	3.1	3.2
Average before-tax income of CU	$54,453.00	$10,923.47	$29,561.76	$44,645.00	$59,259.00	$74,437.00	$88,811.00	$155,901.00
Average spending of CU, total	43,394.87	18,865.37	30,400.94	38,204.07	47,750.13	55,012.03	65,446.39	93,525.67
ALCOHOLIC BEVERAGES	459.27	192.20	291.59	449.21	483.62	617.46	701.51	986.82
Consumed at home	277.59	128.73	188.27	285.91	285.72	368.74	414.54	554.27
Beer and ale	131.31	73.32	116.75	131.99	159.24	180.98	168.44	179.85
Whiskey	21.66	14.31	11.37	29.49	18.58	30.14	21.21	46.93
Wine	94.55	27.81	39.46	103.08	76.79	129.05	170.77	260.23
Other alcoholic beverages	30.07	13.29	20.68	21.35	31.11	28.57	54.12	67.26
Consumed away from home	181.68	63.47	103.33	163.30	197.90	248.71	286.98	432.54
Beer and ale at restaurants, bars	76.32	30.63	47.94	78.57	80.44	104.52	112.18	164.72
Wine at restaurants, bars	22.29	7.05	14.35	22.92	24.98	30.91	36.99	46.39
Whiskey and other alcohol at restaurants, bars	44.71	12.37	24.48	38.17	47.66	68.26	76.21	108.79
Alcoholic beverages purchased on trips	38.37	13.43	16.55	23.64	44.82	45.02	61.60	112.64

Source: Bureau of Labor Statistics, unpublished tables from the 2004 Consumer Expenditure Survey

Table 9. Alcoholic Beverages: Indexed spending by income, 2004

(indexed average annual spending of consumer units (CU) on alcoholic beverages, by before-tax income of consumer unit, 2004; index definition: an index of 100 is the average for all consumer units; an index of 132 means that spending by consumer units in that group is 32 percent above the average for all consumer units; an index of 68 indicates spending that is 32 percent below the average for all consumer units)

	total consumer units	under $20,000	$20,000– $39,999	$40,000– $49,999	$50,000– $69,999	$70,000– $79,999	$80,000– $99,999	$100,000 or more
Average spending of CU, total	$43,395	$18,865	$30,401	$38,204	$47,750	$55,012	$65,446	$93,526
Average spending of CU, index	100	43	70	88	110	127	151	216
ALCOHOLIC BEVERAGES	100	42	63	98	105	134	153	215
Consumed at home	100	46	68	103	103	133	149	200
Beer and ale	100	56	89	101	121	138	128	137
Whiskey	100	66	53	136	86	139	98	217
Wine	100	29	42	109	81	136	181	275
Other alcoholic beverages	100	44	69	71	103	95	180	224
Consumed away from home	100	35	57	90	109	137	158	238
Beer and ale at restaurants, bars	100	40	63	103	105	137	147	216
Wine at restaurants, bars	100	32	64	103	112	139	166	208
Whiskey and other alcohol at restaurants, bars	100	28	55	85	107	153	170	243
Alcoholic beverages purchased on trips	100	35	43	62	117	117	161	294

Source: Calculations by New Strategist based on the Bureau of Labor Statistics 2004 Consumer Expenditure Survey

Table 10. Alcoholic Beverages: Total spending by income, 2004

(total annual spending on alcoholic beverages, by before-tax income group of consumer units (CU), 2004; consumer units and dollars in thousands)

	total consumer units	under $20,000	$20,000–$39,999	$40,000–$49,999	$50,000–$69,999	$70,000–$79,999	$80,000–$99,999	$100,000 or more
Number of consumer units	116,282	28,898	27,297	11,374	18,069	6,461	9,246	14,937
Total spending of all CUs	$5,046,042,273	$545,171,431	$829,854,379	$434,533,092	$862,797,099	$355,432,726	$605,117,322	$1,396,992,933
ALCOHOLIC BEVERAGES	53,404,834	5,554,122	7,959,557	5,109,315	8,738,530	3,989,409	6,486,161	14,740,130
Consumed at home	32,278,720	3,719,987	5,139,229	3,251,940	5,162,675	2,382,429	3,832,837	8,279,131
Beer and ale	15,268,989	2,118,841	3,187,012	1,501,254	2,877,308	1,169,312	1,557,396	2,686,419
Whiskey	2,518,668	413,420	310,456	335,419	335,722	194,735	196,108	700,993
Wine	10,994,463	803,752	1,077,019	1,172,432	1,387,519	833,792	1,578,939	3,887,056
Other alcoholic beverages	3,496,600	384,008	564,470	242,835	562,127	184,591	500,394	1,004,663
Consumed away from home	21,126,114	1,834,063	2,820,470	1,857,374	3,575,855	1,606,915	2,653,417	6,460,850
Beer and ale at restaurants, bars	8,874,642	885,088	1,308,585	893,655	1,453,470	675,304	1,037,216	2,460,423
Wine at restaurants, bars	2,591,926	203,714	391,638	260,692	451,364	199,710	342,010	692,927
Whiskey and other alcohol at restaurants, bars	5,198,968	357,416	668,361	434,146	861,169	441,028	704,638	1,624,996
Alcoholic beverages purchased on trips	4,461,740	387,980	451,886	268,881	809,853	290,874	569,554	1,682,504

Note: Numbers may not add to total because of rounding.
Source: Calculations by New Strategist based on the Bureau of Labor Statistics 2004 Consumer Expenditure Survey

Table 11. Alcoholic Beverages: Market shares by income, 2004

(percentage of total annual spending on alcoholic beverages accounted for by before-tax income group of consumer units, 2004)

	total consumer units	under $20,000	$20,000– $39,999	$40,000– $49,999	$50,000– $69,999	$70,000– $79,999	$80,000– $99,999	$100,000 or more
Share of total consumer units	100.0%	24.9%	23.5%	9.8%	15.5%	5.6%	8.0%	12.8%
Share of total before-tax income	100.0	5.0	12.7	8.0	16.9	7.6	13.0	36.8
Share of total spending	100.0	10.8	16.4	8.6	17.1	7.0	12.0	27.7
ALCOHOLIC BEVERAGES	100.0	10.4	14.9	9.6	16.4	7.5	12.1	27.6
Consumed at home	100.0	11.5	15.9	10.1	16.0	7.4	11.9	25.6
Beer and ale	100.0	13.9	20.9	9.8	18.8	7.7	10.2	17.6
Whiskey	100.0	16.4	12.3	13.3	13.3	7.7	7.8	27.8
Wine	100.0	7.3	9.8	10.7	12.6	7.6	14.4	35.4
Other alcoholic beverages	100.0	11.0	16.1	6.9	16.1	5.3	14.3	28.7
Consumed away from home	100.0	8.7	13.4	8.8	16.9	7.6	12.6	30.6
Beer and ale at restaurants, bars	100.0	10.0	14.7	10.1	16.4	7.6	11.7	27.7
Wine at restaurants, bars	100.0	7.9	15.1	10.1	17.4	7.7	13.2	26.7
Whiskey and other alcohol at restaurants, bars	100.0	6.9	12.9	8.4	16.6	8.5	13.6	31.3
Alcoholic beverages purchased on trips	100.0	8.7	10.1	6.0	18.2	6.5	12.8	37.7

Note: Numbers may not add to total because of rounding.
Source: Calculations by New Strategist based on the Bureau of Labor Statistics 2004 Consumer Expenditure Survey

Table 12. Alcoholic Beverages: Average spending by high-income consumer units, 2004

(average annual spending on alcoholic beverages, by before-tax income of consumer units (CU) with high incomes, 2004)

	total consumer units	$100,000 or more	$100,000– $119,999	$120,000– $149,999	$150,000 or more
Number of consumer units (in 000s)	116,282	14,937	5,625	4,245	5,067
Number of persons per CU	2.5	3.2	3.1	3.3	3.2
Average before-tax income of CU	$54,453.00	$155,901.00	$108,751.00	$132,292.00	$228,021.00
Average spending of CU, total	43,394.87	93,525.67	75,213.14	87,298.57	119,448.79
ALCOHOLIC BEVERAGES	**459.27**	**986.82**	**723.80**	**887.24**	**1,405.43**
Consumed at home	**277.59**	**554.27**	**411.20**	**488.41**	**796.72**
Beer and ale	131.31	179.85	169.04	210.25	162.41
Whiskey	21.66	46.93	38.86	56.15	47.53
Wine	94.55	260.23	164.16	156.29	483.38
Other alcoholic beverages	30.07	67.26	39.14	65.73	103.39
Consumed away from home	**181.68**	**432.54**	**312.60**	**398.82**	**608.72**
Beer and ale at restaurants, bars	76.32	164.72	131.91	135.68	234.40
Wine at restaurants, bars	22.29	46.39	31.80	38.65	72.16
Whiskey and other alcohol at restaurants, bars	44.71	108.79	86.39	108.23	136.90
Alcoholic beverages purchased on trips	38.37	112.64	62.50	116.27	165.26

Source: Bureau of Labor Statistics, unpublished tables from the 2004 Consumer Expenditure Survey

Table 13. Alcoholic Beverages: Indexed spending by high-income consumer units, 2004

(indexed average annual spending of consumer units (CU) with high incomes on alcoholic beverages, by before-tax income of consumer unit, 2004; index definition: an index of 100 is the average for all consumer units; an index of 132 means that spending by consumer units in that group is 32 percent above the average for all consumer units; an index of 68 indicates spending that is 32 percent below the average for all consumer units)

	total consumer units	$100,000 or more	$100,000– $119,999	$120,000– $149,999	$150,000 or more
Average spending of CU, total	$43,395	$93,526	$75,213	$87,299	$119,449
Average spending of CU, index	100	216	173	201	275
ALCOHOLIC BEVERAGES	100	215	158	193	306
Consumed at home	100	200	148	176	287
Beer and ale	100	137	129	160	124
Whiskey	100	217	179	259	219
Wine	100	275	174	165	511
Other alcoholic beverages	100	224	130	219	344
Consumed away from home	100	238	172	220	335
Beer and ale at restaurants, bars	100	216	173	178	307
Wine at restaurants, bars	100	208	143	173	324
Whiskey and other alcohol at restaurants, bars	100	243	193	242	306
Alcoholic beverages purchased on trips	100	294	163	303	431

Source: Calculations by New Strategist based on the Bureau of Labor Statistics 2004 Consumer Expenditure Survey

Table 14. Alcoholic Beverages: Total spending by high-income consumer units, 2004

(total annual spending on alcoholic beverages, by before-tax income group of consumer units (CU) with high incomes, 2004; consumer units and dollars in thousands)

	total consumer units	$100,000 or more	$100,000–$119,999	$120,000–$149,999	$150,000 or more
Number of consumer units	116,282	14,937	5,625	4,245	5,067
Total spending of all CUs	$5,046,042,273	$1,396,992,933	$423,073,913	$370,582,430	$605,247,019
ALCOHOLIC BEVERAGES	53,404,834	14,740,130	4,071,375	3,766,334	7,121,314
Consumed at home	32,278,720	8,279,131	2,313,000	2,073,300	4,036,980
Beer and ale	15,268,989	2,686,419	950,850	892,511	822,931
Whiskey	2,518,668	700,993	218,588	238,357	240,835
Wine	10,994,463	3,887,056	923,400	663,451	2,449,286
Other alcoholic beverages	3,496,600	1,004,663	220,163	279,024	523,877
Consumed away from home	21,126,114	6,460,850	1,758,375	1,692,991	3,084,384
Beer and ale at restaurants, bars	8,874,642	2,460,423	741,994	575,962	1,187,705
Wine at restaurants, bars	2,591,926	692,927	178,875	164,069	365,635
Whiskey and other alcohol at restaurants, bars	5,198,968	1,624,996	485,944	459,436	693,672
Alcoholic beverages purchased on trips	4,461,740	1,682,504	351,563	493,566	837,372

Note: Numbers may not add to total because of rounding.
Source: Calculations by New Strategist based on the Bureau of Labor Statistics 2004 Consumer Expenditure Survey

Table 15. Alcoholic Beverages: Market shares by high-income consumer units, 2004

(percentage of total annual spending on alcoholic beverages accounted for by before-tax income group of consumer units with high incomes, 2004)

	total consumer units	$100,000 or more	$100,000–$119,999	$120,000–$149,999	$150,000 or more
Share of total consumer units	100.0%	12.8%	4.8%	3.7%	4.4%
Share of total before-tax income	100.0	36.8	9.7	8.9	18.2
Share of total spending	100.0	27.7	8.4	7.3	12.0
ALCOHOLIC BEVERAGES	100.0	27.6	7.6	7.1	13.3
Consumed at home	100.0	25.6	7.2	6.4	12.5
Beer and ale	100.0	17.6	6.2	5.8	5.4
Whiskey	100.0	27.8	8.7	9.5	9.6
Wine	100.0	35.4	8.4	6.0	22.3
Other alcoholic beverages	100.0	28.7	6.3	8.0	15.0
Consumed away from home	100.0	30.6	8.3	8.0	14.6
Beer and ale at restaurants, bars	100.0	27.7	8.4	6.5	13.4
Wine at restaurants, bars	100.0	26.7	6.9	6.3	14.1
Whiskey and other alcohol at restaurants, bars	100.0	31.3	9.3	8.8	13.3
Alcoholic beverages purchased on trips	100.0	37.7	7.9	11.1	18.8

Note: Numbers may not add to total because of rounding.
Source: Calculations by New Strategist based on the Bureau of Labor Statistics 2004 Consumer Expenditure Survey

Table 16. Alcoholic Beverages: Average spending by household type, 2004

(average annual spending of consumer units (CU) on alcoholic beverages, by type of consumer unit, 2004)

	total consumer units	total married couples	married couples, no children	married couples with children				single parent, at least one child <18	single person
				total	oldest child under 6	oldest child 6 to 17	oldest child 18 or older		
Number of consumer units (in 000s)	116,282	59,797	25,585	29,279	5,604	15,376	8,300	6,892	33,686
Number of persons per CU	2.5	3.2	2.0	3.9	3.5	4.1	3.9	2.9	1.0
Average before-tax income of CU	$54,453.00	$73,001.00	$64,434.00	$79,764.00	$75,293.00	$78,508.00	$85,109.00	$31,055.00	$28,143.00
Average spending of CU, total	43,394.87	55,606.57	49,690.43	60,660.88	55,981.04	60,577.88	64,161.69	32,824.46	25,423.35
ALCOHOLIC BEVERAGES	459.27	493.23	567.05	442.56	329.70	455.05	505.98	219.37	358.66
Consumed at home	277.59	295.09	316.14	283.71	206.44	307.27	296.58	149.26	200.10
Beer and ale	131.31	135.23	109.10	151.42	119.52	165.69	147.28	82.16	101.71
Whiskey	21.66	21.15	30.96	15.19	12.44	16.11	15.49	6.18	15.84
Wine	94.55	104.86	126.10	93.91	60.35	98.57	111.14	42.52	61.93
Other alcoholic beverages	30.07	33.85	49.98	23.17	14.13	26.89	22.67	18.40	20.63
Consumed away from home	181.68	198.14	250.91	158.86	123.27	147.78	209.40	70.11	158.56
Beer and ale at restaurants, bars	76.32	77.55	95.95	65.83	51.44	59.01	91.62	30.41	76.77
Wine at restaurants, bars	22.29	23.69	32.38	16.96	14.11	16.10	21.02	7.79	18.12
Whiskey and other alcohol at restaurants, bars	44.71	47.32	62.90	36.56	26.20	33.65	50.95	15.94	37.25
Alcoholic beverages purchased on trips	38.37	49.59	59.67	39.51	31.52	39.02	45.81	15.96	26.42

Source: Bureau of Labor Statistics, unpublished tables from the 2004 Consumer Expenditure Survey

Table 17. Alcoholic Beverages: Indexed spending by household type, 2004

(indexed average annual spending of consumer units (CU) on alcoholic beverages, by type of consumer unit, 2004; index definition: an index of 100 is the average for all consumer units; an index of 132 means that spending by consumer units in that group is 32 percent above the average for all consumer units; an index of 68 indicates spending that is 32 percent below the average for all consumer units)

| | total consumer units | total married couples | married couples, no children | married couples with children | | | | single parent, at least one child <18 | single person |
				total	oldest child under 6	oldest child 6 to 17	oldest child 18 or older		
Average spending of CU, total	$43,395	$55,607	$49,690	$60,661	$55,981	$60,578	$64,162	$32,824	$25,423
Average spending of CU, index	100	128	115	140	129	140	148	76	59
ALCOHOLIC BEVERAGES	100	107	123	96	72	99	110	48	78
Consumed at home	100	106	114	102	74	111	107	54	72
Beer and ale	100	103	83	115	91	126	112	63	77
Whiskey	100	98	143	70	57	74	72	29	73
Wine	100	111	133	99	64	104	118	45	65
Other alcoholic beverages	100	113	166	77	47	89	75	61	69
Consumed away from home	100	109	138	87	68	81	115	39	87
Beer and ale at restaurants, bars	100	102	126	86	67	77	120	40	101
Wine at restaurants, bars	100	106	145	76	63	72	94	35	81
Whiskey and other alcohol at restaurants, bars	100	106	141	82	59	75	114	36	83
Alcoholic beverages purchased on trips	100	129	156	103	82	102	119	42	69

Source: Calculations by New Strategist based on the Bureau of Labor Statistics 2004 Consumer Expenditure Survey

Table 18. Alcohol Beverages: Total spending by household type, 2004

(total annual spending on alcoholic beverages, by consumer unit (CU) type, 2002; consumer units and dollars in thousands)

| | total consumer units | total married couples | married couples, no children | married couples with children | | | | single parent, at least one child <18 | single person |
				total	oldest child under 6	oldest child 6 to 17	oldest child 18 or older		
Number of consumer units	116,282	59,797	25,585	29,279	5,604	15,376	8,300	6,892	33,686
Total spending of all CUs	$5,046,042,273	$3,325,106,066	$1,271,329,652	$1,776,089,906	$313,717,748	$931,445,483	$532,542,027	$226,226,178	$856,410,968
ALCOHOLIC BEVERAGES	53,404,834	29,493,674	14,507,974	12,957,714	1,847,639	6,996,849	4,199,634	1,511,898	12,081,821
Consumed at home	32,278,720	17,645,497	8,088,442	8,306,745	1,156,890	4,724,584	2,461,614	1,028,700	6,740,569
Beer and ale	15,268,989	8,086,348	2,791,324	4,433,426	669,790	2,547,649	1,222,424	566,247	3,426,203
Whiskey	2,518,668	1,264,707	792,112	444,748	69,714	247,707	128,567	42,593	533,586
Wine	10,994,463	6,270,313	3,226,269	2,749,591	338,201	1,515,612	922,462	293,048	2,086,174
Other alcoholic beverages	3,496,600	2,024,128	1,278,738	678,394	79,185	413,461	188,161	126,813	694,942
Consumed away from home	21,126,114	11,848,178	6,419,532	4,651,262	690,805	2,272,265	1,738,020	483,198	5,341,252
Beer and ale at restaurants, bars	8,874,642	4,637,257	2,454,881	1,927,437	288,270	907,338	760,446	209,586	2,586,074
Wine at restaurants, bars	2,591,926	1,416,591	828,442	496,572	79,072	247,554	174,466	53,689	610,390
Whiskey, other alcohol at restaurants, bars	5,198,968	2,829,594	1,609,297	1,070,440	146,825	517,402	422,885	109,858	1,254,804
Alcoholic beverages purchased on trips	4,461,740	2,965,333	1,526,657	1,156,813	176,638	599,972	380,223	109,996	889,984

Note: Numbers will not add to total because not all types of consumer units are shown.
Source: Calculations by New Strategist based on the Bureau of Labor Statistics 2004 Consumer Expenditure Survey

Table 19. Alcoholic Beverages: Market shares by household type, 2004

(percentage of total annual spending on alcoholic beverages accounted for by types of consumer units, 2004)

| | total consumer units | total married couples | married couples, no children | married couples with children | | | | single parent, at least one child <18 | single person |
				total	oldest child under 6	oldest child 6 to 17	oldest child 18 or older		
Share of total consumer units	100.0%	51.4%	22.0%	25.2%	4.8%	13.2%	7.1%	5.9%	29.0%
Share of total before-tax income	100.0	68.9	26.0	36.9	6.7	19.1	11.2	3.4	15.0
Share of total spending	100.0	65.9	25.2	35.2	6.2	18.5	10.6	4.5	17.0
ALCOHOLIC BEVERAGES	100.0	55.2	27.2	24.3	3.5	13.1	7.9	2.8	22.6
Consumed at home	100.0	54.7	25.1	25.7	3.6	14.6	7.6	3.2	20.9
Beer and ale	100.0	53.0	18.3	29.0	4.4	16.7	8.0	3.7	22.4
Whiskey	100.0	50.2	31.4	17.7	2.8	9.8	5.1	1.7	21.2
Wine	100.0	57.0	29.3	25.0	3.1	13.8	8.4	2.7	19.0
Other alcoholic beverages	100.0	57.9	36.6	19.4	2.3	11.8	5.4	3.6	19.9
Consumed away from home	100.0	56.1	30.4	22.0	3.3	10.8	8.2	2.3	25.3
Beer and ale at restaurants, bars	100.0	52.3	27.7	21.7	3.2	10.2	8.6	2.4	29.1
Wine at restaurants, bars	100.0	54.7	32.0	19.2	3.1	9.6	6.7	2.1	23.5
Whiskey and other alcohol at restaurants, bars	100.0	54.4	31.0	20.6	2.8	10.0	8.1	2.1	24.1
Alcoholic beverages purchased on trips	100.0	66.5	34.2	25.9	4.0	13.4	8.5	2.5	19.9

Note: Market shares by type of consumer unit will not add to total because not all types of consumer units are shown.
Source: Calculations by New Strategist based on the Bureau of Labor Statistics 2004 Consumer Expenditure Survey

Table 20. Alcoholic Beverages: Average spending by race and Hispanic origin, 2004

(average annual spending of consumer units (CU) on alcoholic beverages, by race and Hispanic origin of consumer unit reference person, 2004)

	total consumer units	Asian	black	Hispanic	non-Hispanic white and other
Number of consumer units (in 000s)	116,282	3,957	13,773	12,298	90,424
Number of persons per CU	2.5	2.8	2.6	3.3	2.3
Average before-tax income of CU	$54,453.00	$67,705.00	$38,503.00	$43,693.00	$58,314.00
Average spending of CU, total	43,394.87	49,458.68	30,481.49	37,578.03	46,163.26
ALCOHOLIC BEVERAGES	459.27	325.05	171.14	320.35	522.81
Consumed at home	277.59	148.83	112.28	220.15	311.00
Beer and ale	131.31	61.83	61.14	163.56	137.46
Whiskey	21.66	18.00	16.34	8.27	24.33
Wine	94.55	64.51	22.72	29.06	114.87
Other alcoholic beverages	30.07	4.49	12.08	19.26	34.35
Consumed away from home	181.68	176.22	58.87	100.20	211.80
Beer and ale at restaurants, bars	76.32	74.04	24.16	42.16	89.16
Wine at restaurants, bars	22.29	25.66	6.79	12.50	26.04
Whiskey and other alcohol at restaurants, bars	44.71	50.13	17.54	24.17	51.74
Alcoholic beverages purchased on trips	38.37	26.39	10.38	21.37	44.86

Note: "Asian" and "black" include Hispanics and non-Hispanics who identify themselves as being of the respective race alone. "Hispanic" includes people of any race who identify themselves as Hispanic. "Other" includes people who identify themselves as non-Hispanic and as Alaska Native, American Indian, Asian (who are also included in the "Asian" column), Native Hawaiian or other Pacific Islander, as well as non-Hispanics reporting more than one race.
Source: Bureau of Labor Statistics, unpublished tables from the 2004 Consumer Expenditure Survey

Table 21. Alcoholic Beverages: Indexed spending by race and Hispanic origin, 2004

(indexed average annual spending of consumer units (CU) on alcoholic beverages, by race and Hispanic origin of consumer unit reference person, 2004; index definition: an index of 100 is the average for all consumer units; an index of 132 means that spending by consumer units in that group is 32 percent above the average for all consumer units; an index of 68 indicates spending that is 32 percent below the average for all consumer units)

	total consumer units	Asian	black	Hispanic	non-Hispanic white and other
Average spending of CU, total	$43,395	$49,459	$30,481	$37,578	$46,163
Average spending of CU, index	100	114	70	87	106
ALCOHOLIC BEVERAGES	100	71	37	70	114
Consumed at home	100	54	40	79	112
Beer and ale	100	47	47	125	105
Whiskey	100	83	75	38	112
Wine	100	68	24	31	121
Other alcoholic beverages	100	15	40	64	114
Consumed away from home	100	97	32	55	117
Beer and ale at restaurants, bars	100	97	32	55	117
Wine at restaurants, bars	100	115	30	56	117
Whiskey and other alcohol at restaurants, bars	100	112	39	54	116
Alcoholic beverages purchased on trips	100	69	27	56	117

Note: "Asian" and "black" include Hispanics and non-Hispanics who identify themselves as being of the respective race alone. "Hispanic" includes people of any race who identify themselves as Hispanic. "Other" includes people who identify themselves as non-Hispanic and as Alaska Native, American Indian, Asian (who are also included in the "Asian" column), Native Hawaiian or other Pacific Islander, as well as non-Hispanics reporting more than one race. Source: Calculations by New Strategist based on the Bureau of Labor Statistics 2004 Consumer Expenditure Survey

Table 22. Alcoholic Beverages: Total spending by race and Hispanic origin, 2004

(total annual spending on alcoholic beverages, by consumer unit race and Hispanic origin groups, 2004; consumer units and dollars in thousands)

	total consumer units	Asian	black	Hispanic	non-Hispanic white and other
Number of consumer units	116,282	3,957	13,773	12,298	90,424
Total spending of all consumer units	$5,046,042,273	$195,707,997	$419,821,562	$462,134,613	$4,174,266,622
ALCOHOLIC BEVERAGES	53,404,834	1,286,223	2,357,111	3,939,664	47,274,571
Consumed at home	32,278,720	588,920	1,546,432	2,707,405	28,121,864
Beer and ale	15,268,989	244,661	842,081	2,011,461	12,429,683
Whiskey	2,518,668	71,226	225,051	101,704	2,200,016
Wine	10,994,463	255,266	312,923	357,380	10,387,005
Other alcoholic beverages	3,496,600	17,767	166,378	236,859	3,106,064
Consumed away from home	21,126,114	697,303	810,817	1,232,260	19,151,803
Beer and ale at restaurants, bars	8,874,642	292,976	332,756	518,484	8,062,204
Wine at restaurants, bars	2,591,926	101,537	93,519	153,725	2,354,641
Whiskey and other alcohol at restaurants, bars	5,198,968	198,364	241,578	297,243	4,678,538
Alcoholic beverages purchased on trips	4,461,740	104,425	142,964	262,808	4,056,421

Note: "Asian" and "black" include Hispanics and non-Hispanics who identify themselves as being of the respective race alone. "Hispanic" includes people of any race who identify themselves as Hispanic. "Other" includes people who identify themselves as non-Hispanic and as Alaska Native, American Indian, Asian (who are also included in the "Asian" column), Native Hawaiian or other Pacific Islander, as well as non-Hispanics reporting more than one race. Numbers may not add to total because of rounding.
Source: Calculations by New Strategist based on the Bureau of Labor Statistics 2004 Consumer Expenditure Survey

Table 23. Alcoholic Beverages: Market shares by race and Hispanic origin, 2004

(percentage of total annual spending on alcoholic beverages accounted for by consumer unit race and Hispanic origin groups, 2004)

	total consumer units	Asian	black	Hispanic	non-Hispanic white and other
Share of total consumer units	100.0%	3.4%	11.8%	10.6%	77.8%
Share of total before-tax income	100.0	4.2	8.4	8.5	83.3
Share of total spending	100.0	3.9	8.3	9.2	82.7
ALCOHOLIC BEVERAGES	100.0	2.4	4.4	7.4	88.5
Consumed at home	100.0	1.8	4.8	8.4	87.1
Beer and ale	100.0	1.6	5.5	13.2	81.4
Whiskey	100.0	2.8	8.9	4.0	87.3
Wine	100.0	2.3	2.8	3.3	94.5
Other alcoholic beverages	100.0	0.5	4.8	6.8	88.8
Consumed away from home	100.0	3.3	3.8	5.8	90.7
Beer and ale at restaurants, bars	100.0	3.3	3.7	5.8	90.8
Wine at restaurants, bars	100.0	3.9	3.6	5.9	90.8
Whiskey and other alcohol at restaurants, bars	100.0	3.8	4.6	5.7	90.0
Alcoholic beverages purchased on trips	100.0	2.3	3.2	5.9	90.9

Note: "Asian" and "black" include Hispanics and non-Hispanics who identify themselves as being of the respective race alone. "Hispanic" includes people of any race who identify themselves as Hispanic. "Other" includes people who identify themselves as non-Hispanic and as Alaska Native, American Indian, Asian (who are also included in the "Asian" column), Native Hawaiian or other Pacific Islander, as well as non-Hispanics reporting more than one race.
Source: Calculations by New Strategist based on the 2002 Consumer Expenditure Survey

Table 24. Alcoholic Beverages: Average spending by region, 2004

(average annual spending of consumer units (CU) on alcoholic beverages, by region in which consumer unit lives, 2004)

	total consumer units	Northeast	Midwest	South	West
Number of consumer units (in 000s)	116,282	22,051	26,539	41,801	25,891
Number of persons per CU	2.5	2.4	2.4	2.5	2.6
Average before-tax income of CU	$54,453.00	$61,050.00	$53,567.00	$50,775.00	$55,682.00
Average spending of CU, total	43,394.87	46,114.89	43,370.77	39,173.65	47,921.74
ALCOHOLIC BEVERAGES	459.27	624.80	426.63	347.55	532.22
Consumed at home	277.59	373.63	233.69	225.19	325.84
Beer and ale	131.31	138.19	130.43	120.67	143.63
Whiskey	21.66	25.47	17.88	22.15	21.52
Wine	94.55	172.81	60.42	57.79	122.45
Other alcoholic beverages	30.07	37.17	24.96	24.58	38.23
Consumed away from home	181.68	251.17	192.94	122.36	206.38
Beer and ale at restaurants, bars	76.32	108.98	88.29	47.64	82.30
Wine at restaurants, bars	22.29	29.96	23.49	15.54	25.41
Whiskey and other alcohol at restaurants, bars	44.71	71.27	43.17	30.86	45.92
Alcoholic beverages purchased on trips	38.37	40.96	37.98	28.33	52.76

Source: Bureau of Labor Statistics, unpublished tables from the 2004 Consumer Expenditure Survey

Table 25. Alcoholic Beverages: Indexed spending by region, 2004

(indexed average annual spending of consumer units (CU) on alcoholic beverages, by region in which consumer unit lives, 2004; index definition: an index of 100 is the average for all consumer units; an index of 132 means that spending by consumer units in that group is 32 percent above the average for all consumer units; an index of 68 indicates spending that is 32 percent below the average for all consumer units)

	total consumer units	Northeast	Midwest	South	West
Average spending of CU, total	$43,395	$46,115	$43,371	$39,174	$47,922
Average spending of CU, index	100	106	100	90	110
ALCOHOLIC BEVERAGES	100	136	93	76	116
Consumed at home	100	135	84	81	117
Beer and ale	100	105	99	92	109
Whiskey	100	118	83	102	99
Wine	100	183	64	61	130
Other alcoholic beverages	100	124	83	82	127
Consumed away from home	100	138	106	67	114
Beer and ale at restaurants, bars	100	143	116	62	108
Wine at restaurants, bars	100	134	105	70	114
Whiskey and other alcohol at restaurants, bars	100	159	97	69	103
Alcoholic beverages purchased on trips	100	107	99	74	138

Source: Calculations by New Strategist based on the Bureau of Labor Statistics 2004 Consumer Expenditure Survey

Table 26. Alcoholic Beverages: Total spending by region, 2004

(total annual spending on alcoholic beverages, by region in which consumer unit lives, 2004; consumer units and dollars in thousands)

	total consumer units	Northeast	Midwest	South	West
Number of consumer units	116,282	22,051	26,539	41,801	25,891
Total spending of all consumer units	$5,046,042,273	$1,016,879,439	$1,151,016,865	$1,637,497,744	$1,240,741,770
ALCOHOLIC BEVERAGES	53,404,834	13,777,465	11,322,334	14,527,938	13,779,708
Consumed at home	32,278,720	8,238,915	6,201,899	9,413,167	8,436,323
Beer and ale	15,268,989	3,047,228	3,461,482	5,044,127	3,718,724
Whiskey	2,518,668	561,639	474,517	925,892	557,174
Wine	10,994,463	3,810,633	1,603,486	2,415,680	3,170,353
Other alcoholic beverages	3,496,600	819,636	662,413	1,027,469	989,813
Consumed away from home	21,126,114	5,538,550	5,120,435	5,114,770	5,343,385
Beer and ale at restaurants, bars	8,874,642	2,403,118	2,343,128	1,991,400	2,130,829
Wine at restaurants, bars	2,591,926	660,648	623,401	649,588	657,890
Whiskey and other alcohol at restaurants, bars	5,198,968	1,571,575	1,145,689	1,289,979	1,188,915
Alcoholic beverages purchased on trips	4,461,740	903,209	1,007,951	1,184,222	1,366,009

Note: Numbers may not add to total because of rounding.
Source: Calculations by New Strategist based on the Bureau of Labor Statistics 2004 Consumer Expenditure Survey

Table 27. Alcoholic Beverages: Market shares by region, 2004

(percentage of total annual spending on alcoholic beverages accounted for by consumer units by region, 2004)

	total consumer units	Northeast	Midwest	South	West
Share of total consumer units	100.0%	19.0%	22.8%	35.9%	22.3%
Share of total before-tax income	100.0	21.3	22.5	33.5	22.8
Share of total spending	100.0	20.2	22.8	32.5	24.6
ALCOHOLIC BEVERAGES	100.0	25.8	21.2	27.2	25.8
Consumed at home	100.0	25.5	19.2	29.2	26.1
Beer and ale	100.0	20.0	22.7	33.0	24.4
Whiskey	100.0	22.3	18.8	36.8	22.1
Wine	100.0	34.7	14.6	22.0	28.8
Other alcoholic beverages	100.0	23.4	18.9	29.4	28.3
Consumed away from home	100.0	26.2	24.2	24.2	25.3
Beer and ale at restaurants, bars	100.0	27.1	26.4	22.4	24.0
Wine at restaurants, bars	100.0	25.5	24.1	25.1	25.4
Whiskey and other alcohol at restaurants, bars	100.0	30.2	22.0	24.8	22.9
Alcoholic beverages purchased on trips	100.0	20.2	22.6	26.5	30.6

Note: Numbers may not add to total because of rounding.
Source: Calculations by New Strategist based on the Bureau of Labor Statistics 2004 Consumer Expenditure Survey

Table 28. Alcoholic Beverages: Average spending by education, 2004

(average annual spending of consumer units (CU) on alcoholic beverages, by education of consumer unit reference person, 2004)

	total consumer units	less than high school graduate	high school graduate	some college	associate's degree	college graduate total	bachelor's degree	master's, professional, doctorate
Number of consumer units (in 000s)	116,282	16,829	31,005	25,317	10,678	32,452	20,684	11,768
Number of persons per CU	2.5	2.7	2.5	2.3	2.6	2.5	2.4	2.5
Average before-tax income of CU	$54,453.00	$29,094.00	$42,334.00	$46,756.00	$58,593.00	$83,825.00	$75,647.00	$98,201.00
Average spending of CU, total	43,394.87	25,421.18	35,438.55	40,877.68	48,177.36	60,712.28	56,728.41	67,801.38
ALCOHOLIC BEVERAGES	459.27	201.70	344.92	451.72	447.93	711.05	692.80	745.51
Consumed at home	277.59	156.37	225.81	275.73	278.29	390.95	362.66	444.96
Beer and ale	131.31	113.40	135.95	141.53	149.87	123.14	132.81	104.68
Whiskey	21.66	11.48	14.11	27.49	16.07	31.75	26.70	41.38
Wine	94.55	19.73	55.72	69.44	81.33	192.26	162.56	248.95
Other alcoholic beverages	30.07	11.76	20.03	37.27	31.02	43.80	40.58	49.95
Consumed away from home	181.68	45.33	119.11	175.99	169.64	320.11	330.13	300.55
Beer and ale at restaurants, bars	76.32	21.79	51.90	76.23	71.93	129.28	134.44	119.44
Wine at restaurants, bars	22.29	6.04	16.08	23.40	17.88	37.16	40.98	29.88
Whiskey and other alcohol at restaurants, bars	44.71	9.47	29.27	41.90	43.45	80.09	83.85	72.91
Alcoholic beverages purchased on trips	38.37	8.03	21.86	34.47	36.37	73.57	70.87	78.32

Source: Bureau of Labor Statistics, unpublished tables from the 2004 Consumer Expenditure Survey

Table 29. Alcoholic Beverages: Indexed spending by education, 2004

(indexed average annual spending of consumer units (CU) on alcoholic beverages, by education of consumer unit reference person, 2004; index definition: an index of 100 is the average for all consumer units; an index of 132 means that spending by consumer units in that group is 32 percent above the average for all consumer units; an index of 68 indicates spending that is 32 percent below the average for all consumer units)

	total consumer units	less than high school graduate	high school graduate	some college	associate's degree	college graduate total	bachelor's degree	master's, professional, doctorate
Average spending of CU, total	$43,395	$25,421	$35,439	$40,878	$48,177	$60,712	$56,728	$67,801
Average spending of CU, index	100	59	82	94	111	140	131	156
ALCOHOLIC BEVERAGES	**100**	**44**	**75**	**98**	**98**	**155**	**151**	**162**
Consumed at home	**100**	**56**	**81**	**99**	**100**	**141**	**131**	**160**
Beer and ale	100	86	104	108	114	94	101	80
Whiskey	100	53	65	127	74	147	123	191
Wine	100	21	59	73	86	203	172	263
Other alcoholic beverages	100	39	67	124	103	146	135	166
Consumed away from home	**100**	**25**	**66**	**97**	**93**	**176**	**182**	**165**
Beer and ale at restaurants, bars	100	29	68	100	94	169	176	156
Wine at restaurants, bars	100	27	72	105	80	167	184	134
Whiskey and other alcohol at restaurants, bars	100	21	65	94	97	179	188	163
Alcoholic beverages purchased on trips	100	21	57	90	95	192	185	204

Source: Calculations by New Strategist based on the Bureau of Labor Statistics 2004 Consumer Expenditure Survey

Table 30. Alcoholic Beverages: Total spending by education, 2004

(total annual spending on alcoholic beverages, by education of consumer unit (CU) reference person, 2004; consumer units and dollars in thousands)

	total consumer units	less than high school graduate	high school graduate	some college	associate's degree	college graduate total	bachelor's degree	master's, professional, doctorate
Number of consumer units	116,282	16,829	31,005	25,317	10,678	32,452	20,684	11,768
Total spending of all CUs	$5,046,042,273	$427,813,038	$1,098,772,243	$1,034,900,225	$514,437,850	$1,970,234,911	$1,173,370,432	$797,886,640
ALCOHOLIC BEVERAGES	53,404,834	3,394,409	10,694,245	11,436,195	4,782,997	23,074,995	14,329,875	8,773,162
Consumed at home	32,278,720	2,631,551	7,001,239	6,980,656	2,971,581	12,687,109	7,501,259	5,236,289
Beer and ale	15,268,989	1,908,409	4,215,130	3,583,115	1,600,312	3,996,139	2,747,042	1,231,874
Whiskey	2,518,668	193,197	437,481	695,964	171,595	1,030,351	552,263	486,960
Wine	10,994,463	332,036	1,727,599	1,758,012	868,442	6,239,222	3,362,391	2,929,644
Other alcoholic beverages	3,496,600	197,909	621,030	943,565	331,232	1,421,398	839,357	587,812
Consumed away from home	21,126,114	762,859	3,693,006	4,455,539	1,811,416	10,388,210	6,828,409	3,536,872
Beer and ale at restaurants, bars	8,874,642	366,704	1,609,160	1,929,915	768,069	4,195,395	2,780,757	1,405,570
Wine at restaurants, bars	2,591,926	101,647	498,560	592,418	190,923	1,205,916	847,630	351,628
Whiskey and other alcohol at restaurants, bars	5,198,968	159,371	907,516	1,060,782	463,959	2,599,081	1,734,353	858,005
Alcoholic beverages purchased on trips	4,461,740	135,137	677,769	872,677	388,359	2,387,494	1,465,875	921,670

Note: Numbers may not add to total because of rounding.
Source: Calculations by New Strategist based on the Bureau of Labor Statistics 2004 Consumer Expenditure Survey

Table 31. Alcoholic Beverages: Market shares by education, 2004

(percentage of total annual spending on alcoholic beverages accounted for by education of consumer unit reference person, 2004)

	total consumer units	less than high school graduate	high school graduate	some college	associate's degree	college graduate		
						total	bachelor's degree	master's, professional, doctorate
Share of total consumer units	100.0%	14.5%	26.7%	21.8%	9.2%	27.9%	17.8%	10.1%
Share of total before-tax income	100.0	7.7	20.7	18.7	9.9	43.0	24.7	18.3
Share of total spending	100.0	8.5	21.8	20.5	10.2	39.0	23.3	15.8
ALCOHOLIC BEVERAGES	100.0	6.4	20.0	21.4	9.0	43.2	26.8	16.4
Consumed at home	100.0	8.2	21.7	21.6	9.2	39.3	23.2	16.2
Beer and ale	100.0	12.5	27.6	23.5	10.5	26.2	18.0	8.1
Whiskey	100.0	7.7	17.4	27.6	6.8	40.9	21.9	19.3
Wine	100.0	3.0	15.7	16.0	7.9	56.7	30.6	26.6
Other alcoholic beverages	100.0	5.7	17.8	27.0	9.5	40.7	24.0	16.8
Consumed away from home	100.0	3.6	17.5	21.1	8.6	49.2	32.3	16.7
Beer and ale at restaurants, bars	100.0	4.1	18.1	21.7	8.7	47.3	31.3	15.8
Wine at restaurants, bars	100.0	3.9	19.2	22.9	7.4	46.5	32.7	13.6
Whiskey and other alcohol at restaurants, bars	100.0	3.1	17.5	20.4	8.9	50.0	33.4	16.5
Alcoholic beverages purchased on trips	100.0	3.0	15.2	19.6	8.7	53.5	32.9	20.7

Note: Numbers may not add to total because of rounding.
Source: Calculations by New Strategist based on the Bureau of Labor Statistics 2004 Consumer Expenditure Survey

Alcoholic Beverages Purchased on Trips

Best customers:	Householders aged 45 to 64
	High-income households
	Married couples without children at home
	College graduates
Customer trends:	Spending in this category is likely to grow as boomers enter the peak spending age group—if discretionary income rises.

The biggest spenders on alcoholic beverages purchased on trips are older travelers. Householders aged 45 to 64 spend 15 to 28 percent more than average on this item. High-income households spend nearly three times the average and control 38 percent of the market. Married couples without children at home spend 56 percent more than the average household on alcoholic beverages while on trips. Most of them are empty-nesters, who spend more on travel than other household types. Empty-nesters also spend more on alcoholic beverages than couples with children at home.

Average household spending on alcoholic beverages purchased on trips climbed only 2 percent between 2000 and 2004, after adjusting for inflation. This increase is much smaller than the gains made in any other alcoholic beverage category during those years. Behind the small rise is the overall reduction in travel following the September 11, 2001 terrorist attacks. Average household spending on alcoholic beverages on trips should grow as boomers enter the peak spending age group—if discretionary income rises.

Table 32. Alcoholic beverages purchased on trips

Total household spending	$4,461,740,340.00
Average household spends	38.37

	AVERAGE HOUSEHOLD SPENDING	BEST CUSTOMERS (index)	BIGGEST CUSTOMERS (market share)
AGE OF HOUSEHOLDER			
Average household	**$38.37**	**100**	**100.0%**
Under age 25	26.73	70	5.3
Aged 25 to 34	39.93	104	17.4
Aged 35 to 44	38.92	101	21.0
Aged 45 to 54	44.08	115	23.4
Aged 55 to 64	49.04	128	19.2
Aged 65 to 74	37.40	97	9.4
Aged 75 or older	16.49	43	4.3

	AVERAGE HOUSEHOLD SPENDING	BEST CUSTOMERS (index)	BIGGEST CUSTOMERS (market share)
HOUSEHOLD INCOME			
Average household	**$38.37**	**100**	**100.0%**
Under $20,000	13.43	35	8.7
$20,000 to $39,999	16.55	43	10.1
$40,000 to $49,999	23.64	62	6.0
$50,000 to $69,999	44.82	117	18.2
$70,000 to $79,999	45.02	117	6.5
$80,000 to $99,999	61.60	161	12.8
$100,000 or more	112.64	294	37.7
HOUSEHOLD TYPE			
Average household	**38.37**	**100**	**100.0**
Married couples	49.59	129	66.5
Married couples, no children	59.67	156	34.2
Married couples, with children	39.51	103	25.9
Oldest child under 6	31.52	82	4.0
Oldest child 6 to 17	39.02	102	13.4
Oldest child 18 or older	45.81	119	8.5
Single parent with child under 18	15.96	42	2.5
Single person	26.42	69	19.9
RACE AND HISPANIC ORIGIN			
Average household	**38.37**	**100**	**100.0**
Asian	26.39	69	2.3
Black	10.38	27	3.2
Hispanic	21.37	56	5.9
Non-Hispanic white and other	44.86	117	90.9
REGION			
Average household	**38.37**	**100**	**100.0**
Northeast	40.96	107	20.2
Midwest	37.98	99	22.6
South	28.33	74	26.5
West	52.76	138	30.6
EDUCATION			
Average household	**38.37**	**100**	**100.0**
Less than high school graduate	8.03	21	3.0
High school graduate	21.86	57	15.2
Some college	34.47	90	19.6
Associate's degree	36.37	95	8.7
College graduate	73.57	192	53.5
Bachelor's degree	70.87	185	32.9
Master's, professional, doctoral degree	78.32	204	20.7

Note: Market shares may not sum to 100.0 because of rounding and missing categories by household type. "Asian" and "black" include Hispanics and non-Hispanics who identify themselves as being of the respective race alone. "Hispanic" includes people of any race who identify themselves as Hispanic. "Other" includes people who identify themselves as non-Hispanic and as Alaska Native, American Indian, Asian (who are also included in the "Asian" row), Native Hawaiian or other Pacific Islander, as well as non-Hispanics reporting more than one race.
Source: Calculations by New Strategist based on the Bureau of Labor Statistics 2004 Consumer Expenditure Survey

Beer and Ale at Home

Best customers:
Householders under age 45
Married couples with school-aged children
Hispanics

Customer trends:
Spending is likely to increase as the large millennial generation fills the 25-to-44 age group.

Householders under age 45 spend 32 to 39 percent more than the average household on beer and ale consumed at home, making them the best customers of this product. Householders under age 25, many of whom just reached legal drinking age, spend the most—39 percent more than average. Married couples with school-aged children spend 26 percent more than average on this item. Hispanics spend 25 percent more.

Average household spending on beer and ale consumed at home increased 7 percent between 2000 and 2004, after adjusting for inflation. As the large millennial generation ages into its late twenties and thirties (the oldest were aged 27 in 2004), household spending on beer and ale consumed at home is likely to climb simply because more households will be in the big-spending age groups.

Table 33. **Beer and ale at home**

Total household spending $15,268,989,420.00
Average household spends 131.31

	AVERAGE HOUSEHOLD SPENDING	BEST CUSTOMERS (index)	BIGGEST CUSTOMERS (market share)
AGE OF HOUSEHOLDER			
Average household	$131.31	100	100.0%
Under age 25	182.80	139	10.6
Aged 25 to 34	182.57	139	23.2
Aged 35 to 44	172.98	132	27.3
Aged 45 to 54	132.46	101	20.6
Aged 55 to 64	93.87	71	10.7
Aged 65 to 74	55.45	42	4.1
Aged 75 or older	37.72	29	2.8

	AVERAGE HOUSEHOLD SPENDING	BEST CUSTOMERS (index)	BIGGEST CUSTOMERS (market share)
HOUSEHOLD INCOME			
Average household	**$131.31**	**100**	**100.0%**
Under $20,000	73.32	56	13.9
$20,000 to $39,999	116.75	89	20.9
$40,000 to $49,999	131.99	101	9.8
$50,000 to $69,999	159.24	121	18.8
$70,000 to $79,999	180.98	138	7.7
$80,000 to $99,999	168.44	128	10.2
$100,000 or more	179.85	137	17.6
HOUSEHOLD TYPE			
Average household	**131.31**	**100**	**100.0**
Married couples	135.23	103	53.0
Married couples, no children	109.10	83	18.3
Married couples, with children	151.42	115	29.0
Oldest child under 6	119.52	91	4.4
Oldest child 6 to 17	165.69	126	16.7
Oldest child 18 or older	147.28	112	8.0
Single parent with child under 18	82.16	63	3.7
Single person	101.71	77	22.4
RACE AND HISPANIC ORIGIN			
Average household	**131.31**	**100**	**100.0**
Asian	61.83	47	1.6
Black	61.14	47	5.5
Hispanic	163.56	125	13.2
Non-Hispanic white and other	137.46	105	81.4
REGION			
Average household	**131.31**	**100**	**100.0**
Northeast	138.19	105	20.0
Midwest	130.43	99	22.7
South	120.67	92	33.0
West	143.63	109	24.4
EDUCATION			
Average household	**131.31**	**100**	**100.0**
Less than high school graduate	113.40	86	12.5
High school graduate	135.95	104	27.6
Some college	141.53	108	23.5
Associate's degree	149.87	114	10.5
College graduate	123.14	94	26.2
Bachelor's degree	132.81	101	18.0
Master's, professional, doctoral degree	104.68	80	8.1

Note: Market shares may not sum to 100.0 because of rounding and missing categories by household type. "Asian" and "black" include Hispanics and non-Hispanics who identify themselves as being of the respective race alone. "Hispanic" includes people of any race who identify themselves as Hispanic. "Other" includes people who identify themselves as non-Hispanic and as Alaska Native, American Indian, Asian (who are also included in the "Asian" row), Native Hawaiian or other Pacific Islander, as well as non-Hispanics reporting more than one race.
Source: Calculations by New Strategist based on the Bureau of Labor Statistics 2004 Consumer Expenditure Survey

Beer and Ale at Restaurants and Bars

Best customers: Householders under age 35
                           Married couples without children at home
                           Households in the Northeast
                           College graduates

Customer trends: Spending should increase as empty-nesters head a growing proportion of
                           households.

Householders under age 35 are the best customers of beer and ale at restaurants and bars, spending 34 to 40 percent more than the average household on this item. Married couples without children at home, many of them empty-nesters, spend 26 percent more than the average household on this item. Households in the Northeast spend 43 percent more. Households headed by college graduates, who also have the highest incomes, spend 69 percent more than average on this item.

Average household spending on beer and ale consumed at restaurants and bars increased 11 percent between 2000 and 2004, after adjusting for inflation. Behind the increase in spending on alcoholic beverages overall, and this category in particular, is the growing number of households headed by empty-nesters. With more boomers becoming empty-nesters as their children leave home, spending on alcoholic beverages should continue to rise.

Table 34. Beer and ale at restaurants and bars

Total household spending $8,874,642,240.00
Average household spends   76.32

	AVERAGE HOUSEHOLD SPENDING	BEST CUSTOMERS (index)	BIGGEST CUSTOMERS (market share)
AGE OF HOUSEHOLDER			
Average household	**$76.32**	**100**	**100.0%**
Under age 25	102.53	134	10.2
Aged 25 to 34	106.75	140	23.4
Aged 35 to 44	68.69	90	18.6
Aged 45 to 54	88.64	116	23.7
Aged 55 to 64	69.58	91	13.7
Aged 65 to 74	49.59	65	6.3
Aged 75 or older	28.45	37	3.7

	AVERAGE HOUSEHOLD SPENDING	BEST CUSTOMERS (index)	BIGGEST CUSTOMERS (market share)
HOUSEHOLD INCOME			
Average household	**$76.32**	**100**	**100.0%**
Under $20,000	30.63	40	10.0
$20,000 to $39,999	47.94	63	14.7
$40,000 to $49,999	78.57	103	10.1
$50,000 to $69,999	80.44	105	16.4
$70,000 to $79,999	104.52	137	7.6
$80,000 to $99,999	112.18	147	11.7
$100,000 or more	164.72	216	27.7
HOUSEHOLD TYPE			
Average household	**76.32**	**100**	**100.0**
Married couples	77.55	102	52.3
Married couples, no children	95.95	126	27.7
Married couples, with children	65.83	86	21.7
Oldest child under 6	51.44	67	3.2
Oldest child 6 to 17	59.01	77	10.2
Oldest child 18 or older	91.62	120	8.6
Single parent with child under 18	30.41	40	2.4
Single person	76.77	101	29.1
RACE AND HISPANIC ORIGIN			
Average household	**76.32**	**100**	**100.0**
Asian	74.04	97	3.3
Black	24.16	32	3.7
Hispanic	42.16	55	5.8
Non-Hispanic white and other	89.16	117	90.8
REGION			
Average household	**76.32**	**100**	**100.0**
Northeast	108.98	143	27.1
Midwest	88.29	116	26.4
South	47.64	62	22.4
West	82.30	108	24.0
EDUCATION			
Average household	**76.32**	**100**	**100.0**
Less than high school graduate	21.79	29	4.1
High school graduate	51.90	68	18.1
Some college	76.23	100	21.7
Associate's degree	71.93	94	8.7
College graduate	129.28	169	47.3
Bachelor's degree	134.44	176	31.3
Master's, professional, doctoral degree	119.44	156	15.8

Note: Market shares may not sum to 100.0 because of rounding and missing categories by household type. "Asian" and "black" include Hispanics and non-Hispanics who identify themselves as being of the respective race alone. "Hispanic" includes people of any race who identify themselves as Hispanic. "Other" includes people who identify themselves as non-Hispanic and as Alaska Native, American Indian, Asian (who are also included in the "Asian" row), Native Hawaiian or other Pacific Islander, as well as non-Hispanics reporting more than one race.
Source: Calculations by New Strategist based on the Bureau of Labor Statistics 2004 Consumer Expenditure Survey

Whiskey and Other Alcohol at Home

Best customers:	Married couples without children at home
	College graduates
Customer trends:	Spending is likely to increase as empty-nesters and the college educated become a larger share of the population.

Married couples without children at home spend 43 percent more than the average household on whiskey and other alcohol consumed at home. College graduates spend 47 percent more than average on this item, with spending rising as high as 91 percent above average for those with graduate-level degrees.

Average household spending on whiskey and other alcohol consumed at home has grown substantially (up 36 percent) since 2000, after adjusting for inflation. Behind the increase is the growth of the demographic segments that spend more on alcohol—empty-nesters and college graduates. Spending on this item is likely to continue to grow along with these demographic segments.

Table 35. Whiskey and other alcohol (except beer and wine) at home

Total household spending	$2,518,668,120.00
Average household spends	21.66

	AVERAGE HOUSEHOLD SPENDING	BEST CUSTOMERS (index)	BIGGEST CUSTOMERS (market share)
AGE OF HOUSEHOLDER			
Average household	**$21.66**	**100**	**100.0%**
Under age 25	24.54	113	8.6
Aged 25 to 34	11.95	55	9.2
Aged 35 to 44	26.93	124	25.7
Aged 45 to 54	21.55	99	20.3
Aged 55 to 64	26.69	123	18.5
Aged 65 to 74	23.09	107	10.3
Aged 75 or older	15.94	74	7.3

	AVERAGE HOUSEHOLD SPENDING	BEST CUSTOMERS (index)	BIGGEST CUSTOMERS (market share)
HOUSEHOLD INCOME			
Average household	**$21.66**	**100**	**100.0%**
Under $20,000	14.31	66	16.4
$20,000 to $39,999	11.37	53	12.3
$40,000 to $49,999	29.49	136	13.3
$50,000 to $69,999	18.58	86	13.3
$70,000 to $79,999	30.14	139	7.7
$80,000 to $99,999	21.21	98	7.8
$100,000 or more	46.93	217	27.8
HOUSEHOLD TYPE			
Average household	**21.66**	**100**	**100.0**
Married couples	21.15	98	50.2
Married couples, no children	30.96	143	31.4
Married couples, with children	15.19	70	17.7
Oldest child under 6	12.44	57	2.8
Oldest child 6 to 17	16.11	74	9.8
Oldest child 18 or older	15.49	72	5.1
Single parent with child under 18	6.18	29	1.7
Single person	15.84	73	21.2
RACE AND HISPANIC ORIGIN			
Average household	**21.66**	**100**	**100.0**
Asian	18.00	83	2.8
Black	16.34	75	8.9
Hispanic	8.27	38	4.0
Non-Hispanic white and other	24.33	112	87.3
REGION			
Average household	**21.66**	**100**	**100.0**
Northeast	25.47	118	22.3
Midwest	17.88	83	18.8
South	22.15	102	36.8
West	21.52	99	22.1
EDUCATION			
Average household	**21.66**	**100**	**100.0**
Less than high school graduate	11.48	53	7.7
High school graduate	14.11	65	17.4
Some college	27.49	127	27.6
Associate's degree	16.07	74	6.8
College graduate	31.75	147	40.9
Bachelor's degree	26.70	123	21.9
Master's, professional, doctoral degree	41.38	191	19.3

Note: Market shares may not sum to 100.0 because of rounding and missing categories by household type. "Asian" and "black" include Hispanics and non-Hispanics who identify themselves as being of the respective race alone. "Hispanic" includes people of any race who identify themselves as Hispanic. "Other" includes people who identify themselves as non-Hispanic and as Alaska Native, American Indian, Asian (who are also included in the "Asian" row), Native Hawaiian or other Pacific Islander, as well as non-Hispanics reporting more than one race.
Source: Calculations by New Strategist based on the Bureau of Labor Statistics 2004 Consumer Expenditure Survey

Whiskey and Other Alcohol at Restaurants and Bars

Best customers:	**Householders under age 35**
	Married couples without children at home
	Households in the Northeast
	College graduates
Customer trends:	**Spending is likely to increase as empty-nesters and college graduates become a larger share of the population.**

Householders under age 35 spend 41 to 43 percent more than the average household on whiskey and other alcohol consumed at restaurants and bars. Couples without children at home, most of them empty-nesters, spend 41 percent more. Households in the Northeast spend 59 percent more than average on this item, and college graduates spend 79 percent more.

Average household spending on whiskey and other alcohol consumed at restaurants and bars climbed a substantial 33 percent between 2000 and 2004, after adjusting for inflation. Behind the increase is the growth of the demographic segments that spend more on alcohol—empty-nesters and college graduates. Spending on this item is likely to continue to grow along with these demographic segments.

Table 36. Whiskey and other alcohol (except beer and wine) at restaurants and bars

Total household spending	$5,198,968,220.00
Average household spends	44.71

	AVERAGE HOUSEHOLD SPENDING	BEST CUSTOMERS (index)	BIGGEST CUSTOMERS (market share)
AGE OF HOUSEHOLDER			
Average household	**$44.71**	**100**	**100.0%**
Under age 25	62.90	141	10.7
Aged 25 to 34	63.87	143	23.9
Aged 35 to 44	44.28	99	20.5
Aged 45 to 54	48.82	109	22.3
Aged 55 to 64	38.24	86	12.9
Aged 65 to 74	26.82	60	5.8
Aged 75 or older	15.83	35	3.5

	AVERAGE HOUSEHOLD SPENDING	BEST CUSTOMERS (index)	BIGGEST CUSTOMERS (market share)
HOUSEHOLD INCOME			
Average household	**$44.71**	**100**	**100.0%**
Under $20,000	12.37	28	6.9
$20,000 to $39,999	24.48	55	12.9
$40,000 to $49,999	38.17	85	8.4
$50,000 to $69,999	47.66	107	16.6
$70,000 to $79,999	68.26	153	8.5
$80,000 to $99,999	76.21	170	13.6
$100,000 or more	108.79	243	31.3
HOUSEHOLD TYPE			
Average household	**44.71**	**100**	**100.0**
Married couples	47.32	106	54.4
Married couples, no children	62.90	141	31.0
Married couples, with children	36.56	82	20.6
Oldest child under 6	26.20	59	2.8
Oldest child 6 to 17	33.65	75	10.0
Oldest child 18 or older	50.95	114	8.1
Single parent with child under 18	15.94	36	2.1
Single person	37.25	83	24.1
RACE AND HISPANIC ORIGIN			
Average household	**44.71**	**100**	**100.0**
Asian	50.13	112	3.8
Black	17.54	39	4.6
Hispanic	24.17	54	5.7
Non-Hispanic white and other	51.74	116	90.0
REGION			
Average household	**44.71**	**100**	**100.0**
Northeast	71.27	159	30.2
Midwest	43.17	97	22.0
South	30.86	69	24.8
West	45.92	103	22.9
EDUCATION			
Average household	**44.71**	**100**	**100.0**
Less than high school graduate	9.47	21	3.1
High school graduate	29.27	65	17.5
Some college	41.90	94	20.4
Associate's degree	43.45	97	8.9
College graduate	80.09	179	50.0
Bachelor's degree	83.85	188	33.4
Master's, professional, doctoral degree	72.91	163	16.5

Note: Market shares may not sum to 100.0 because of rounding and missing categories by household type. "Asian" and "black" include Hispanics and non-Hispanics who identify themselves as being of the respective race alone. "Hispanic" includes people of any race who identify themselves as Hispanic. "Other" includes people who identify themselves as non-Hispanic and as Alaska Native, American Indian, Asian (who are also included in the "Asian" row), Native Hawaiian or other Pacific Islander, as well as non-Hispanics reporting more than one race.
Source: Calculations by New Strategist based on the Bureau of Labor Statistics 2004 Consumer Expenditure Survey

Wine at Home

Best customers: Householders aged 35 to 64
                                        Married couples without children at home
                                        Households in the Northeast and West
                                        College graduates

Customer trends: Spending will continue to increase as a growing proportion of boomers enter the empty-nest lifestage, when spending on alcoholic beverages rises.

Wine has a reputation for being the alcoholic beverage of choice among the elite. The demographics of wine's best customers bear that out. Those who spend the most on wine consumed at home, college graduates, spend more than twice the average on this item. Married couples without children at home, many of them empty-nesters, spend 33 percent more than average on this item. Boomers are known for their penchant for wine, which may explain why householders aged 35 to 64 spend 18 to 43 percent more than average on wine consumed at home. Households in the Northeast and West also spend much more than average on this item.

Average household spending on wine consumed at home has grown 8 percent since 2000, after adjusting for inflation. One factor behind the increase is the aging of the highly educated baby-boom generation into the empty-nest lifestage, when spending on alcoholic beverages increases. Spending on wine at home will continue to grow as more boomers become empty-nesters.

Table 37. Wine at home

Total household spending $10,994,463,100.00
Average household spends   94.55

	AVERAGE HOUSEHOLD SPENDING	BEST CUSTOMERS (index)	BIGGEST CUSTOMERS (market share)
AGE OF HOUSEHOLDER			
Average household	**$94.55**	**100**	**100.0%**
Under age 25	38.62	41	3.1
Aged 25 to 34	59.49	63	10.5
Aged 35 to 44	135.56	143	29.7
Aged 45 to 54	111.59	118	24.1
Aged 55 to 64	115.32	122	18.3
Aged 65 to 74	92.66	98	9.5
Aged 75 or older	45.09	48	4.7

	AVERAGE HOUSEHOLD SPENDING	BEST CUSTOMERS (index)	BIGGEST CUSTOMERS (market share)
HOUSEHOLD INCOME			
Average household	**$94.55**	**100**	**100.0%**
Under $20,000	27.81	29	7.3
$20,000 to $39,999	39.46	42	9.8
$40,000 to $49,999	103.08	109	10.7
$50,000 to $69,999	76.79	81	12.6
$70,000 to $79,999	129.05	136	7.6
$80,000 to $99,999	170.77	181	14.4
$100,000 or more	260.23	275	35.4
HOUSEHOLD TYPE			
Average household	**94.55**	**100**	**100.0**
Married couples	104.86	111	57.0
Married couples, no children	126.10	133	29.3
Married couples, with children	93.91	99	25.0
Oldest child under 6	60.35	64	3.1
Oldest child 6 to 17	98.57	104	13.8
Oldest child 18 or older	111.14	118	8.4
Single parent with child under 18	42.52	45	2.7
Single person	61.93	65	19.0
RACE AND HISPANIC ORIGIN			
Average household	**94.55**	**100**	**100.0**
Asian	64.51	68	2.3
Black	22.72	24	2.8
Hispanic	29.06	31	3.3
Non-Hispanic white and other	114.87	121	94.5
REGION			
Average household	**94.55**	**100**	**100.0**
Northeast	172.81	183	34.7
Midwest	60.42	64	14.6
South	57.79	61	22.0
West	122.45	130	28.8
EDUCATION			
Average household	**94.55**	**100**	**100.0**
Less than high school graduate	19.73	21	3.0
High school graduate	55.72	59	15.7
Some college	69.44	73	16.0
Associate's degree	81.33	86	7.9
College graduate	192.26	203	56.7
Bachelor's degree	162.56	172	30.6
Master's, professional, doctoral degree	248.95	263	26.6

Note: Market shares may not sum to 100.0 because of rounding and missing categories by household type. "Asian" and "black" include Hispanics and non-Hispanics who identify themselves as being of the respective race alone. "Hispanic" includes people of any race who identify themselves as Hispanic. "Other" includes people who identify themselves as non-Hispanic and as Alaska Native, American Indian, Asian (who are also included in the "Asian" row), Native Hawaiian or other Pacific Islander, as well as non-Hispanics reporting more than one race.
Source: Calculations by New Strategist based on the Bureau of Labor Statistics 2004 Consumer Expenditure Survey

Wine at Restaurants and Bars

Best customers:	Householders under age 35
	Married couples without children at home
	Households in the Northeast
	College graduates
Customer trends:	Spending will continue to increase as more boomers enter the empty-nest lifestage, when household spending at full-service restaurants rises.

The best customers of wine consumed at restaurants and bars are young adults and householders with the time and money to relax with a glass of wine, perhaps over a meal. Those who spend the most on wine at restaurants and bars are adults under age 35 and married couples without children at home (many are empty-nesters). These household types spend 33 to 46 percent more than average on this item. Households in the Northeast spend 34 percent more than average on this item. Those headed by college graduates also spend well above average on wine at restaurants and bars because they can afford to do so.

Average household spending on wine at restaurants and bars grew by 14 percent between 2000 and 2004, after adjusting for inflation. One factor behind the increase is the entry of the baby-boom generation into the empty-nest lifestage, when spending on full-service restaurants and alcoholic beverages increases. Spending on this item will continue to climb for the next decade as a growing proportion of boomers become empty-nesters.

Table 38. Wine at restaurants and bars

Total household spending $2,591,925,780.00
Average household spends   22.29

	AVERAGE HOUSEHOLD SPENDING	BEST CUSTOMERS (index)	BIGGEST CUSTOMERS (market share)
AGE OF HOUSEHOLDER			
Average household	**$22.29**	**100**	**100.0%**
Under age 25	32.57	146	11.1
Aged 25 to 34	29.61	133	22.2
Aged 35 to 44	19.29	87	17.9
Aged 45 to 54	25.68	115	23.5
Aged 55 to 64	20.67	93	13.9
Aged 65 to 74	15.80	71	6.8
Aged 75 or older	9.28	42	4.1

	AVERAGE HOUSEHOLD SPENDING	BEST CUSTOMERS (index)	BIGGEST CUSTOMERS (market share)
HOUSEHOLD INCOME			
Average household	**$22.29**	**100**	**100.0%**
Under $20,000	7.05	32	7.9
$20,000 to $39,999	14.35	64	15.1
$40,000 to $49,999	22.92	103	10.1
$50,000 to $69,999	24.98	112	17.4
$70,000 to $79,999	30.91	139	7.7
$80,000 to $99,999	36.99	166	13.2
$100,000 or more	46.39	208	26.7
HOUSEHOLD TYPE			
Average household	**22.29**	**100**	**100.0**
Married couples	23.69	106	54.7
Married couples, no children	32.38	145	32.0
Married couples, with children	16.96	76	19.2
Oldest child under 6	14.11	63	3.1
Oldest child 6 to 17	16.10	72	9.6
Oldest child 18 or older	21.02	94	6.7
Single parent with child under 18	7.79	35	2.1
Single person	18.12	81	23.5
RACE AND HISPANIC ORIGIN			
Average household	**22.29**	**100**	**100.0**
Asian	25.66	115	3.9
Black	6.79	30	3.6
Hispanic	12.50	56	5.9
Non-Hispanic white and other	26.04	117	90.8
REGION			
Average household	**22.29**	**100**	**100.0**
Northeast	29.96	134	25.5
Midwest	23.49	105	24.1
South	15.54	70	25.1
West	25.41	114	25.4
EDUCATION			
Average household	**22.29**	**100**	**100.0**
Less than high school graduate	6.04	27	3.9
High school graduate	16.08	72	19.2
Some college	23.40	105	22.9
Associate's degree	17.88	80	7.4
College graduate	37.16	167	46.5
Bachelor's degree	40.98	184	32.7
Master's, professional, doctoral degree	29.88	134	13.6

Note: Market shares may not sum to 100.0 because of rounding and missing categories by household type. "Asian" and "black" include Hispanics and non-Hispanics who identify themselves as being of the respective race alone. "Hispanic" includes people of any race who identify themselves as Hispanic. "Other" includes people who identify themselves as non-Hispanic and as Alaska Native, American Indian, Asian (who are also included in the "Asian" row), Native Hawaiian or other Pacific Islander, as well as non-Hispanics reporting more than one race.
Source: Calculations by New Strategist based on the Bureau of Labor Statistics 2004 Consumer Expenditure Survey

Household Spending on Nonalcoholic Beverages, 2004

Between 2000 and 2004, average household spending on nonalcoholic beverages purchased at grocery and convenience stores fell slightly, down 0.9 percent, after adjusting for inflation.

Carbonated drinks are the nonalcoholic beverage category on which households spend the most—an average of $142 in 2004. This is 4 percent less than in 2000, however, after adjusting for inflation. Milk is the second-largest nonalcoholic beverage category, with the average household spending $129 on milk in 2004—2 percent less than in 2000. Spending on fruit juice fell 16 percent, with frozen fruit juice experiencing a 45 percent decline. Increased spending on restaurant breakfasts may be behind the fruit juice decline.

Average household spending on coffee fell 17 percent between 2000 and 2004. The decline in the at-home consumption of coffee may be caused by the proliferation of Starbucks and other coffee outlets. Coffee has been battling with colas for the caffeine-addicted market, and these numbers suggest it may be losing the battle.

The biggest spending increase in the nonalcoholic beverage category occurred for "other nonalcoholic beverages and ice." The average household boosted its spending on this category by 68 percent between 2000 and 2004, after adjusting for inflation. Included in the category are sports drinks, which are less widely available at restaurants and carry-outs, and bottled water.

Spending by age

The biggest spenders on nonalcoholic beverages are the largest households. Householders aged 35 to 54—the age when household size peaks—spent more than $600 on nonalcoholic beverages from grocery and convenience stores in 2004, fully 18 to 21 percent more than the $510 spent by the average household. Householders aged 35 to 44 are especially big spenders on fruit-flavored drinks and account for 30 percent of the market. Householders aged 45 to 64 spend the most on roasted coffee, 23 to 41 percent more than average.

Spending by household income

Spending on nonalcoholic beverages rises with income. Households with incomes of $100,000 or more spend 50 percent more than the average household on this category. They spend 67 percent more than average on roasted coffee. Households with incomes below $40,000 spend less than average on almost every type of nonalcoholic beverage.

Spending by household type

Married couples with school-aged or older children at home are the best customers of nonalcoholic beverages purchased from grocery and convenience stores, spending 50 to 51 percent more than the average household on these items. They spend more than average on every type of nonalcoholic beverage. Because their household size is smaller, married couples without children at home (most of them empty-nesters) spend less than average on a number of beverages, but they are above-average spenders on roasted coffee (with an index of 146) and instant coffee (with an index of 139). Single parents spend 52 percent more than average on fruit-flavored drinks.

Spending by race and Hispanic origin

Black households spend 18 percent less than the average household on nonalcoholic beverages, but they spend 43 percent more than average on fruit-flavored drinks. Asian households spend 7 percent less than average on the nonalcoholic beverage category, but they spend 18 percent more than average on tea. Hispanics, who have the largest households, spend 24 percent more than average on nonalcoholic beverages overall. They are the best customers of milk.

Spending by region

Spending on nonalcoholic beverages varies somewhat by region, with households in the West spending the most ($558 in 2004). Households in the Northeast spend the most on tea (with an index of 129). Households in the Midwest are the biggest spenders on carbonated drinks. Households in the West are the best customers of roasted coffee.

Spending by education

Spending on nonalcoholic beverages rises slightly with education. College graduates spend 6 percent more than the average household on the category, while those who went no further than high school spend 3 percent less than average. College graduates are big spenders on some items, however. They spend 18 percent more than average on roasted coffee and 29 percent more than average on fresh fruit juice.

Table 39. Nonalcoholic Beverage Spending, 2000 to 2004

(average annual and percent distribution of household spending on nonalcoholic beverages, 2000 to 2004; percent change in spending, 2000–04; in 2004 dollars)

	2004		2000		
	average household spending	percent distribution	average household spending (in 2004$)	percent distribution	percent change 2000–04
Total spending on nonalcoholic beverages	**$509.94**	**100.0%**	**$514.39**	**100.0%**	**–0.9%**
Carbonated drinks	141.89	27.8	147.41	28.7	–3.7
Colas	93.81	18.4	95.43	18.6	–1.7
Noncolas	48.08	9.4	51.99	10.1	–7.5
Milk, fresh	128.94	25.3	131.21	25.5	–1.7
Fruit juice	83.56	16.4	99.16	19.3	–15.7
Canned and bottled	55.05	10.8	61.66	12.0	–10.7
Fresh	22.07	4.3	25.71	5.0	–14.2
Frozen	6.44	1.3	11.78	2.3	–45.3
Other nonalcoholic beverages and ice	70.10	13.7	41.67	8.1	68.2
Coffee	38.08	7.5	45.91	8.9	–17.1
Roasted	24.48	4.8	30.17	5.9	–18.9
Instant and freeze-dried	14.64	2.9	15.74	3.1	–7.0
Fruit-flavored drinks	19.79	3.9	21.30	4.1	–7.1
Tea	17.63	3.5	17.20	3.3	2.5
Vegetable juice	8.91	1.7	10.52	2.0	–15.3

Source: Bureau of Labor Statistics, 2000 and 2004 Consumer Expenditure Surveys; calculations by New Strategist

Table 40. Nonalcoholic Beverages: Average spending by age, 2004

(average annual spending of consumer units (CU) on nonalcoholic beverages, by age of consumer unit reference person, 2004)

	total consumer units	under 25	25 to 34	35 to 44	45 to 54	55 to 64	65 to 74	75+
Number of consumer units (in 000s)	116,282	28,898	27,297	11,374	18,069	6,461	9,246	14,937
Number of persons per CU	2.5	1.8	2.3	2.6	2.8	3.0	3.1	3.2
Average before-tax income of CU	$54,453.00	$10,923.47	$29,561.76	$44,645.00	$59,259.00	$74,437.00	$88,811.00	$155,901.00
Average spending of CU, total	43,394.87	18,865.37	30,400.94	38,204.07	47,750.13	55,012.03	65,446.39	93,525.67
NONALCOHOLIC BEVERAGES	**509.94**	**308.93**	**509.75**	**602.18**	**618.57**	**501.96**	**416.58**	**346.32**
Carbonated drinks, colas	93.81	55.21	90.96	107.59	118.84	104.63	73.88	49.98
Carbonated drinks, noncolas	48.08	34.14	44.15	57.97	61.06	50.43	35.20	26.47
Coffee, instant and freeze-dried	14.64	4.98	10.04	14.26	21.55	16.19	14.55	14.68
Coffee, roasted	24.48	6.71	17.86	23.18	34.60	29.99	27.78	20.22
Fruit-flavored drinks	19.79	16.46	23.24	28.62	21.58	15.78	12.15	6.93
Fruit juice, canned and bottled	55.05	39.67	59.48	61.11	64.52	48.92	46.75	44.15
Fruit juice, fresh	22.07	9.88	23.45	24.17	25.68	25.09	19.44	15.14
Fruit juice, frozen	6.44	4.64	5.78	7.42	6.49	5.66	5.65	8.90
Milk, fresh	128.94	79.18	132.79	159.16	143.87	120.21	109.30	97.47
Tea	17.63	13.24	14.75	18.96	23.28	19.36	14.91	11.54
Vegetable juice	8.91	4.83	7.93	10.31	10.49	7.92	10.48	7.42
Other nonalcoholic beverages and ice	70.10	39.99	79.32	89.43	86.61	57.78	46.49	43.42

Source: Bureau of Labor Statistics, unpublished tables from the 2004 Consumer Expenditure Survey

Table 41. Nonalcoholic Beverages: Indexed spending by age, 2004

(indexed average annual spending of consumer units (CU) on nonalcoholic beverages, by age of consumer unit reference person, 2004; index definition: an index of 100 is the average for all consumer units; an index of 132 means that spending by consumer units in that group is 32 percent above the average for all consumer units; an index of 68 indicates spending that is 32 percent below the average for all consumer units)

	total consumer units	under 25	25 to 34	35 to 44	45 to 54	55 to 64	65 to 74	75+
Average spending of CU, total	$43,395	$18,865	$30,401	$38,204	$47,750	$55,012	$65,446	$93,526
Average spending of CU, index	100	43	70	88	110	127	151	216
NONALCOHOLIC BEVERAGES	100	61	100	118	121	98	82	68
Carbonated drinks, colas	100	59	97	115	127	112	79	53
Carbonated drinks, noncolas	100	71	92	121	127	105	73	55
Coffee, instant and freeze-dried	100	34	69	97	147	111	99	100
Coffee, roasted	100	27	73	95	141	123	113	83
Fruit-flavored drinks	100	83	117	145	109	80	61	35
Fruit juice, canned and bottled	100	72	108	111	117	89	85	80
Fruit juice, fresh	100	45	106	110	116	114	88	69
Fruit juice, frozen	100	72	90	115	101	88	88	138
Milk, fresh	100	61	103	123	112	93	85	76
Tea	100	75	84	108	132	110	85	65
Vegetable juice	100	54	89	116	118	89	118	83
Other nonalcoholic beverages and ice	100	57	113	128	124	82	66	62

Source: Calculations by New Strategist based on the Bureau of Labor Statistics 2004 Consumer Expenditure Survey

Table 42. Nonalcoholic Beverages: Total spending by age, 2004

(total annual spending on nonalcoholic beverages, by consumer unit (CU) age group, 2004; consumer units and dollars in thousands)

	total consumer units	under 25	25 to 34	35 to 44	45 to 54	55 to 64	65 to 74	75+
Number of consumer units	116,282	28,898	27,297	11,374	18,069	6,461	9,246	14,937
Total spending of all CUs	$5,046,042,273	$545,171,431	$829,854,379	$434,533,092	$862,797,099	$355,432,726	$605,117,322	$1,396,992,933
NONALCOHOLIC BEVERAGES	**59,296,843**	**2,723,836**	**9,909,030**	**14,494,473**	**14,667,532**	**8,773,759**	**4,678,193**	**3,995,148**
Carbonated drinks, colas	10,908,414	486,787	1,768,171	2,589,691	2,817,934	1,828,828	829,672	576,569
Carbonated drinks, noncolas	5,590,839	301,012	858,232	1,395,338	1,447,855	881,466	395,296	305,358
Coffee, instant and freeze-dried	1,702,368	43,909	195,168	343,238	510,994	282,985	163,397	169,348
Coffee, roasted	2,846,583	59,162	347,181	557,943	820,435	524,195	311,969	233,258
Fruit-flavored drinks	2,301,221	145,128	451,762	688,883	511,705	275,819	136,445	79,944
Fruit juice, canned and bottled	6,401,324	349,770	1,156,232	1,470,918	1,529,898	855,073	525,003	509,314
Fruit juice, fresh	2,566,344	87,112	455,845	581,772	608,924	438,548	218,311	174,655
Fruit juice, frozen	748,856	40,911	112,357	178,599	153,891	98,931	63,450	102,670
Milk, fresh	14,993,401	698,130	2,581,305	3,830,981	3,411,445	2,101,151	1,227,439	1,124,414
Tea	2,050,052	116,737	286,725	456,367	552,015	338,393	167,439	133,125
Vegetable juice	1,036,073	42,586	154,151	248,162	248,739	138,434	117,690	85,597
Other nonalcoholic beverages and ice	8,151,368	352,592	1,541,901	2,152,580	2,053,696	1,009,937	522,083	500,893

Note: Numbers may not add to total because of rounding.
Source: Calculations by New Strategist based on the Bureau of Labor Statistics 2004 Consumer Expenditure Survey

Table 43. Nonalcoholic Beverages: Market shares by age, 2004

(percentage of total annual spending on nonalcoholic beverages accounted for by consumer unit age groups, 2004)

	total consumer units	under 25	25 to 34	35 to 44	45 to 54	55 to 64	65 to 74	75+
Share of total consumer units	100.0%	24.9%	23.5%	9.8%	15.5%	5.6%	8.0%	12.8%
Share of total before-tax income	100.0	5.0	12.7	8.0	16.9	7.6	13.0	36.8
Share of total spending	100.0	10.8	16.4	8.6	17.1	7.0	12.0	27.7
NONALCOHOLIC BEVERAGES	100.0	4.6	16.7	24.4	24.7	14.8	7.9	6.7
Carbonated drinks, colas	100.0	4.5	16.2	23.7	25.8	16.8	7.6	5.3
Carbonated drinks, noncolas	100.0	5.4	15.4	25.0	25.9	15.8	7.1	5.5
Coffee, instant and freeze-dried	100.0	2.6	11.5	20.2	30.0	16.6	9.6	9.9
Coffee, roasted	100.0	2.1	12.2	19.6	28.8	18.4	11.0	8.2
Fruit-flavored drinks	100.0	6.3	19.6	29.9	22.2	12.0	5.9	3.5
Fruit juice, canned and bottled	100.0	5.5	18.1	23.0	23.9	13.4	8.2	8.0
Fruit juice, fresh	100.0	3.4	17.8	22.7	23.7	17.1	8.5	6.8
Fruit juice, frozen	100.0	5.5	15.0	23.8	20.6	13.2	8.5	13.7
Milk, fresh	100.0	4.7	17.2	25.6	22.8	14.0	8.2	7.5
Tea	100.0	5.7	14.0	22.3	26.9	16.5	8.2	6.5
Vegetable juice	100.0	4.1	14.9	24.0	24.0	13.4	11.4	8.3
Other nonalcoholic beverages and ice	100.0	4.3	18.9	26.4	25.2	12.4	6.4	6.1

Note: Numbers may not add to total because of rounding.
Source: Calculations by New Strategist based on the Bureau of Labor Statistics 2004 Consumer Expenditure Survey

Table 44. Nonalcoholic Beverages: Average spending by income, 2004

(average annual spending on nonalcoholic beverages, by before-tax income of consumer units (CU), 2004)

	total consumer units	under $20,000	$20,000– $39,999	$40,000– $49,999	$50,000– $69,999	$70,000– $79,999	$80,000– $99,999	$100,000 or more
Number of consumer units (in 000s)	116,282	28,898	27,297	11,374	18,069	6,461	9,246	14,937
Number of persons per CU	2.5	1.8	2.3	2.6	2.8	3.0	3.1	3.2
Average before-tax income of CU	$54,453.00	$10,923.47	$29,561.76	$44,645.00	$59,259.00	$74,437.00	$88,811.00	$155,901.00
Average spending of CU, total	43,394.87	18,865.37	30,400.94	38,204.07	47,750.13	55,012.03	65,446.39	93,525.67
NONALCOHOLIC BEVERAGES	**509.94**	**332.78**	**452.04**	**492.70**	**567.80**	**620.63**	**584.73**	**767.37**
Carbonated drinks, colas	93.81	64.06	88.13	94.73	106.66	105.78	110.48	123.03
Carbonated drinks, noncolas	48.08	29.13	45.66	46.10	54.83	71.38	50.29	67.03
Coffee, instant and freeze-dried	14.64	9.61	12.33	13.21	15.17	23.96	14.69	23.82
Coffee, roasted	24.48	14.54	20.26	20.24	29.19	35.05	27.07	40.88
Fruit-flavored drinks	19.79	13.38	20.20	20.00	22.37	26.57	21.81	22.65
Fruit juice, canned and bottled	55.05	36.32	49.84	51.37	59.48	69.38	59.92	84.62
Fruit juice, fresh	22.07	11.62	19.03	23.28	22.09	22.86	26.91	40.82
Fruit juice, frozen	6.44	4.86	5.70	6.20	7.70	7.02	8.40	7.65
Milk, fresh	128.94	93.50	120.79	128.65	136.51	138.50	147.07	179.41
Tea	17.63	10.84	12.58	16.75	22.61	18.73	18.79	32.26
Vegetable juice	8.91	5.67	8.16	6.41	9.23	11.52	10.13	15.46
Other nonalcoholic beverages and ice	70.10	39.26	49.36	65.76	81.96	89.88	89.17	129.74

Source: Bureau of Labor Statistics, unpublished tables from the 2004 Consumer Expenditure Survey

Table 45. Nonalcoholic Beverages: Indexed spending by income, 2004

(indexed average annual spending of consumer units (CU) on nonalcoholic beverages, by before-tax income of consumer unit, 2004; index definition: an index of 100 is the average for all consumer units; an index of 132 means that spending by consumer units in that group is 32 percent above the average for all consumer units; an index of 68 indicates spending that is 32 percent below the average for all consumer units)

	total consumer units	under $20,000	$20,000– $39,999	$40,000– $49,999	$50,000– $69,999	$70,000– $79,999	$80,000– $99,999	$100,000 or more
Average spending of CU, total	$43,395	$18,865	$30,401	$38,204	$47,750	$55,012	$65,446	$93,526
Average spending of CU, index	100	43	70	88	110	127	151	216
NONALCOHOLIC BEVERAGES	100	65	89	97	111	122	115	150
Carbonated drinks, colas	100	68	94	101	114	113	118	131
Carbonated drinks, noncolas	100	61	95	96	114	148	105	139
Coffee, instant and freeze-dried	100	66	84	90	104	164	100	163
Coffee, roasted	100	59	83	83	119	143	111	167
Fruit-flavored drinks	100	68	102	101	113	134	110	114
Fruit juice, canned and bottled	100	66	91	93	108	126	109	154
Fruit juice, fresh	100	53	86	105	100	104	122	185
Fruit juice, frozen	100	75	89	96	120	109	130	119
Milk, fresh	100	73	94	100	106	107	114	139
Tea	100	61	71	95	128	106	107	183
Vegetable juice	100	64	92	72	104	129	114	174
Other nonalcoholic beverages and ice	100	56	70	94	117	128	127	185

Source: Calculations by New Strategist based on the Bureau of Labor Statistics 2004 Consumer Expenditure Survey

Table 46. Nonalcoholic Beverages: Total spending by income, 2004

(total annual spending on nonalcoholic beverages, by before-tax income group of consumer units (CU), 2004; consumer units and dollars in thousands)

	total consumer units	under $20,000	$20,000–$39,999	$40,000–$49,999	$50,000–$69,999	$70,000–$79,999	$80,000–$99,999	$100,000 or more
Number of consumer units	116,282	28,898	27,297	11,374	18,069	6,461	9,246	14,937
Total spending of all CUs	$5,046,042,273	$545,171,431	$829,854,379	$434,533,092	$862,797,099	$355,432,726	$605,117,322	$1,396,992,933
NONALCOHOLIC BEVERAGES	**59,296,843**	**9,616,759**	**12,339,345**	**5,603,970**	**10,259,578**	**4,009,890**	**5,406,414**	**11,462,206**
Carbonated drinks, colas	10,908,414	1,851,210	2,405,758	1,077,459	1,927,240	683,445	1,021,498	1,837,699
Carbonated drinks, noncolas	5,590,839	841,924	1,246,383	524,341	990,723	461,186	464,981	1,001,227
Coffee, instant and freeze-dried	1,702,368	277,577	336,669	150,251	274,107	154,806	135,824	355,799
Coffee, roasted	2,846,583	420,039	553,114	230,210	527,434	226,458	250,289	610,625
Fruit-flavored drinks	2,301,221	386,709	551,522	227,480	404,204	171,669	201,655	338,323
Fruit juice, canned and bottled	6,401,324	1,049,555	1,360,374	584,282	1,074,744	448,264	554,020	1,263,969
Fruit juice, fresh	2,566,344	335,687	519,424	264,787	399,144	147,698	248,810	609,728
Fruit juice, frozen	748,856	140,468	155,578	70,519	139,131	45,356	77,666	114,268
Milk, fresh	14,993,401	2,701,844	3,297,070	1,463,265	2,466,599	894,849	1,359,809	2,679,847
Tea	2,050,052	313,224	343,486	190,515	408,540	121,015	173,732	481,868
Vegetable juice	1,036,073	163,880	222,612	72,907	166,777	74,431	93,662	230,926
Other nonalcoholic beverages and ice	8,151,368	1,134,643	1,347,356	747,954	1,480,935	580,715	824,466	1,937,926

Note: Numbers may not add to total because of rounding.
Source: Calculations by New Strategist based on the Bureau of Labor Statistics 2004 Consumer Expenditure Survey

Table 47. Nonalcoholic Beverages: Market shares by income, 2004

(percentage of total annual spending on nonalcoholic beverages accounted for by before-tax income group of consumer units, 2004)

	total consumer units	under $20,000	$20,000– $39,999	$40,000– $49,999	$50,000– $69,999	$70,000– $79,999	$80,000– $99,999	$100,000 or more
Share of total consumer units	100.0%	24.9%	23.5%	9.8%	15.5%	5.6%	8.0%	12.8%
Share of total before-tax income	100.0	5.0	12.7	8.0	16.9	7.6	13.0	36.8
Share of total spending	100.0	10.8	16.4	8.6	17.1	7.0	12.0	27.7
NONALCOHOLIC BEVERAGES	100.0	16.2	20.8	9.5	17.3	6.8	9.1	19.3
Carbonated drinks, colas	100.0	17.0	22.1	9.9	17.7	6.3	9.4	16.8
Carbonated drinks, noncolas	100.0	15.1	22.3	9.4	17.7	8.2	8.3	17.9
Coffee, instant and freeze-dried	100.0	16.3	19.8	8.8	16.1	9.1	8.0	20.9
Coffee, roasted	100.0	14.8	19.4	8.1	18.5	8.0	8.8	21.5
Fruit-flavored drinks	100.0	16.8	24.0	9.9	17.6	7.5	8.8	14.7
Fruit juice, canned and bottled	100.0	16.4	21.3	9.1	16.8	7.0	8.7	19.7
Fruit juice, fresh	100.0	13.1	20.2	10.3	15.6	5.8	9.7	23.8
Fruit juice, frozen	100.0	18.8	20.8	9.4	18.6	6.1	10.4	15.3
Milk, fresh	100.0	18.0	22.0	9.8	16.5	6.0	9.1	17.9
Tea	100.0	15.3	16.8	9.3	19.9	5.9	8.5	23.5
Vegetable juice	100.0	15.8	21.5	7.0	16.1	7.2	9.0	22.3
Other nonalcoholic beverages and ice	100.0	13.9	16.5	9.2	18.2	7.1	10.1	23.8

Note: Numbers may not add to total because of rounding.
Source: Calculations by New Strategist based on the Bureau of Labor Statistics 2004 Consumer Expenditure Survey

Table 48. Nonalcoholic Beverages: Average spending by high-income consumer units, 2004

(average annual spending on nonalcoholic beverages, by before-tax income of high-income consumer units (CU), 2004)

	total consumer units	$100,000 or more	$100,000– $119,999	$120,000– $149,999	$150,000 or more
Number of consumer units (in 000s)	116,282	14,937	5,625	4,245	5,067
Number of persons per CU	2.5	3.2	3.1	3.3	3.2
Average before-tax income of CU	$54,453.00	$155,901.00	$108,751.00	$132,292.00	$228,021.00
Average spending of CU, total	43,394.87	93,525.67	75,213.14	87,298.57	119,448.79
NONALCOHOLIC BEVERAGES	**509.94**	**767.37**	**716.39**	**780.70**	**816.56**
Carbonated drinks, colas	93.81	123.03	118.70	133.67	117.62
Carbonated drinks, noncolas	48.08	67.03	62.01	68.90	71.31
Coffee, instant and freeze-dried	14.64	23.82	22.14	20.05	29.71
Coffee, roasted	24.48	40.88	36.98	40.08	46.47
Fruit-flavored drinks	19.79	22.65	21.48	28.62	18.06
Fruit juice, canned and bottled	55.05	84.62	73.33	86.18	96.91
Fruit juice, fresh	22.07	40.82	40.57	33.92	48.09
Fruit juice, frozen	6.44	7.65	7.70	7.90	7.35
Milk, fresh	128.94	179.41	175.51	178.65	184.95
Tea	17.63	32.26	26.77	31.93	39.34
Vegetable juice	8.91	15.46	16.67	14.38	15.06
Other nonalcoholic beverages and ice	70.10	129.74	114.53	136.42	141.69

Source: Bureau of Labor Statistics, unpublished tables from the 2004 Consumer Expenditure Survey

Table 49. Nonalcoholic Beverages: Indexed spending by high-income consumer units, 2004

(indexed average annual spending of high-income consumer units (CU) on nonalcoholic beverages, by before-tax income of consumer unit, 2004; index definition: an index of 100 is the average for all consumer units; an index of 132 means that spending by consumer units in that group is 32 percent above the average for all consumer units; an index of 68 indicates spending that is 32 percent below the average for all consumer units)

	total consumer units	$100,000 or more	$100,000– $119,999	$120,000– $149,999	$150,000 or more
Average spending of CU, total	**$43,395**	**$93,526**	**$75,213**	**$87,299**	**$119,449**
Average spending of CU, index	**100**	**216**	**173**	**201**	**275**
NONALCOHOLIC BEVERAGES	**100**	**150**	**140**	**153**	**160**
Carbonated drinks, colas	100	131	127	142	125
Carbonated drinks, noncolas	100	139	129	143	148
Coffee, instant and freeze-dried	100	163	151	137	203
Coffee, roasted	100	167	151	164	190
Fruit-flavored drinks	100	114	109	145	91
Fruit juice, canned and bottled	100	154	133	157	176
Fruit juice, fresh	100	185	184	154	218
Fruit juice, frozen	100	119	120	123	114
Milk, fresh	100	139	136	139	143
Tea	100	183	152	181	223
Vegetable juice	100	174	187	161	169
Other nonalcoholic beverages and ice	100	185	163	195	202

Source: Calculations by New Strategist based on the Bureau of Labor Statistics 2004 Consumer Expenditure Survey

Table 50. Nonalcoholic Beverages: Total spending by high-income consumer units, 2004

(total annual spending on nonalcoholic beverages, by before-tax income group of high-income consumer units (CU), 2004; consumer units and dollars in thousands)

	total consumer units	$100,000 or more	$100,000– $119,999	$120,000– $149,999	$150,000 or more
Number of consumer units	116,282	14,937	5,625	4,245	5,067
Total spending of all CUs	$5,046,042,273	$1,396,992,933	$423,073,913	$370,582,430	$605,247,019
NONALCOHOLIC BEVERAGES	**59,296,843**	**11,462,206**	**4,029,694**	**3,314,072**	**4,137,510**
Carbonated drinks, colas	10,908,414	1,837,699	667,688	567,429	595,981
Carbonated drinks, noncolas	5,590,839	1,001,227	348,806	292,481	361,328
Coffee, instant and freeze-dried	1,702,368	355,799	124,538	85,112	150,541
Coffee, roasted	2,846,583	610,625	208,013	170,140	235,463
Fruit-flavored drinks	2,301,221	338,323	120,825	121,492	91,510
Fruit juice, canned and bottled	6,401,324	1,263,969	412,481	365,834	491,043
Fruit juice, fresh	2,566,344	609,728	228,206	143,990	243,672
Fruit juice, frozen	748,856	114,268	43,313	33,536	37,242
Milk, fresh	14,993,401	2,679,847	987,244	758,369	937,142
Tea	2,050,052	481,868	150,581	135,543	199,336
Vegetable juice	1,036,073	230,926	93,769	61,043	76,309
Other nonalcoholic beverages and ice	8,151,368	1,937,926	644,231	579,103	717,943

Note: Numbers may not add to total because of rounding.
Source: Calculations by New Strategist based on the Bureau of Labor Statistics 2004 Consumer Expenditure Survey

Table 51. Nonalcoholic Beverages: Market shares by high-income consumer units, 2004

(percentage of total annual spending on nonalcoholic beverages accounted for by before-tax income group of high-income consumer units, 2004)

	total consumer units	$100,000 or more	$100,000– $119,999	$120,000– $149,999	$150,000 or more
Share of total consumer units	100.0%	12.8%	4.8%	3.7%	4.4%
Share of total before-tax income	100.0	36.8	9.7	8.9	18.2
Share of total spending	100.0	27.7	8.4	7.3	12.0
NONALCOHOLIC BEVERAGES	**100.0**	**19.3**	**6.8**	**5.6**	**7.0**
Carbonated drinks, colas	100.0	16.8	6.1	5.2	5.5
Carbonated drinks, noncolas	100.0	17.9	6.2	5.2	6.5
Coffee, instant and freeze-dried	100.0	20.9	7.3	5.0	8.8
Coffee, roasted	100.0	21.5	7.3	6.0	8.3
Fruit-flavored drinks	100.0	14.7	5.3	5.3	4.0
Fruit juice, canned and bottled	100.0	19.7	6.4	5.7	7.7
Fruit juice, fresh	100.0	23.8	8.9	5.6	9.5
Fruit juice, frozen	100.0	15.3	5.8	4.5	5.0
Milk, fresh	100.0	17.9	6.6	5.1	6.3
Tea	100.0	23.5	7.3	6.6	9.7
Vegetable juice	100.0	22.3	9.1	5.9	7.4
Other nonalcoholic beverages and ice	100.0	23.8	7.9	7.1	8.8

Note: Numbers may not add to total because of rounding.
Source: Calculations by New Strategist based on the Bureau of Labor Statistics 2004 Consumer Expenditure Survey

Table 52. Nonalcoholic Beverages: Average spending by household type, 2004

(average annual spending of consumer units (CU) on nonalcoholic beverages, by type of consumer unit, 2004)

| | total consumer units | total married couples | married couples, no children | married couples with children | | | | single parent, at least one child <18 | single person |
				total	oldest child under 6	oldest child 6 to 17	oldest child 18 or older		
Number of consumer units (in 000s)	116,282	59,797	25,585	29,279	5,604	15,376	8,300	6,892	33,686
Number of persons per CU	2.5	3.2	2.0	3.9	3.5	4.1	3.9	2.9	1.0
Average before-tax income of CU	$54,453.00	$73,001.00	$64,434.00	$79,764.00	$75,293.00	$78,508.00	$85,109.00	$31,055.00	$28,143.00
Average spending of CU, total	43,394.87	55,606.57	49,690.43	60,660.88	55,981.04	60,577.88	64,161.69	32,824.46	25,423.35
NONALCOHOLIC BEVERAGES	**509.94**	**640.68**	**503.48**	**727.29**	**578.46**	**764.11**	**769.92**	**488.57**	**268.20**
Carbonated drinks, colas	93.81	115.84	95.17	129.04	96.16	129.91	153.62	88.94	48.80
Carbonated drinks, noncolas	48.08	60.32	44.64	69.39	43.06	72.62	83.78	51.01	24.10
Coffee, instant and freeze-dried	14.64	17.93	20.30	15.90	10.41	16.87	18.30	9.70	9.60
Coffee, roasted	24.48	30.47	35.70	26.43	19.50	27.70	29.34	14.34	15.34
Fruit-flavored drinks	19.79	24.48	13.57	32.54	18.43	40.81	26.61	30.11	8.38
Fruit juice, canned and bottled	55.05	67.29	51.27	76.66	72.45	79.06	75.02	60.87	31.63
Fruit juice, fresh	22.07	27.64	21.31	31.09	23.11	31.06	37.55	18.04	12.03
Fruit juice, frozen	6.44	8.40	6.27	9.84	7.09	10.46	10.73	3.59	3.38
Milk, fresh	128.94	166.56	118.67	198.70	171.98	210.08	196.41	128.33	61.43
Tea	17.63	23.10	22.37	23.25	13.01	22.72	32.60	13.43	9.16
Vegetable juice	8.91	10.99	8.90	12.08	12.42	12.20	11.55	8.47	4.82
Other nonalcoholic beverages and ice	70.10	87.66	65.31	102.37	90.84	110.62	94.41	61.74	39.53

Source: Bureau of Labor Statistics, unpublished tables from the 2004 Consumer Expenditure Survey

Table 53. Nonalcoholic Beverages: Indexed spending by household type, 2004

(indexed average annual spending of consumer units (CU) on nonalcoholic beverages, by type of consumer unit, 2004; index definition: an index of 100 is the average for all consumer units; an index of 132 means that spending by consumer units in that group is 32 percent above the average for all consumer units; an index of 68 indicates spending that is 32 percent below the average for all consumer units)

	total consumer units	total married couples	married couples, no children	married couples with children				single parent, at least one child <18	single person
				total	oldest child under 6	oldest child 6 to 17	oldest child 18 or older		
Average spending of CU, total	$43,395	$55,607	$49,690	$60,661	$55,981	$60,578	$64,162	$32,824	$25,423
Average spending of CU, index	100	128	115	140	129	140	148	76	59
NONALCOHOLIC BEVERAGES	100	126	99	143	113	150	151	96	53
Carbonated drinks, colas	100	123	101	138	103	138	164	95	52
Carbonated drinks, noncolas	100	125	93	144	90	151	174	106	50
Coffee, instant and freeze-dried	100	122	139	109	71	115	125	66	66
Coffee, roasted	100	124	146	108	80	113	120	59	63
Fruit-flavored drinks	100	124	69	164	93	206	134	152	42
Fruit juice, canned and bottled	100	122	93	139	132	144	136	111	57
Fruit juice, fresh	100	125	97	141	105	141	170	82	55
Fruit juice, frozen	100	130	97	153	110	162	167	56	52
Milk, fresh	100	129	92	154	133	163	152	100	48
Tea	100	131	127	132	74	129	185	76	52
Vegetable juice	100	123	100	136	139	137	130	95	54
Other nonalcoholic beverages and ice	100	125	93	146	130	158	135	88	56

Source: Calculations by New Strategist based on the Bureau of Labor Statistics 2004 Consumer Expenditure Survey

Table 54. Nonalcoholic Beverages: Total spending by household type, 2004

(total annual spending on nonalcoholic beverages, by consumer unit (CU) type, 2004; consumer units and dollars in thousands)

	total consumer units	total married couples	married couples, no children	married couples with children				single parent, at least one child <18	single person
				total	oldest child under 6	oldest child 6 to 17	oldest child 18 or older		
Number of consumer units	116,282	59,797	25,585	29,279	5,604	15,376	8,300	6,892	33,686
Total spending of all CUs	$5,046,042,273	$3,325,106,066	$1,271,329,652	$1,776,089,906	$313,717,748	$931,445,483	$532,542,027	$226,226,178	$856,410,968
NONALCOHOLIC BEVERAGES	**59,296,843**	**38,310,742**	**12,881,536**	**21,294,324**	**3,241,690**	**11,748,955**	**6,390,336**	**3,367,224**	**9,034,585**
Carbonated drinks, colas	10,908,414	6,926,884	2,434,924	3,778,162	538,881	1,997,496	1,275,046	612,974	1,643,877
Carbonated drinks, noncolas	5,590,839	3,606,955	1,142,114	2,031,670	241,308	1,116,605	695,374	351,561	811,833
Coffee, instant and freeze-dried	1,702,368	1,072,160	519,376	465,536	58,338	259,393	151,890	66,852	323,386
Coffee, roasted	2,846,583	1,822,015	913,385	773,844	109,278	425,915	243,522	98,831	516,743
Fruit-flavored drinks	2,301,221	1,463,831	347,188	952,739	103,282	627,495	220,863	207,518	282,289
Fruit juice, canned and bottled	6,401,324	4,023,740	1,311,743	2,244,528	406,010	1,215,627	622,666	419,516	1,065,488
Fruit juice, fresh	2,566,344	1,652,789	545,216	910,284	129,508	477,579	311,665	124,332	405,243
Fruit juice, frozen	748,856	502,295	160,418	288,105	39,732	160,833	89,059	24,742	113,859
Milk, fresh	14,993,401	9,959,788	3,036,172	5,817,737	963,776	3,230,190	1,630,203	884,450	2,069,331
Tea	2,050,052	1,381,311	572,336	680,737	72,908	349,343	270,580	92,560	308,564
Vegetable juice	1,036,073	657,169	227,707	353,690	69,602	187,587	95,865	58,375	162,367
Other nonalcoholic beverages and ice	8,151,368	5,241,805	1,670,956	2,997,291	509,067	1,700,893	783,603	425,512	1,331,608

Note: Spending by type of consumer unit will not add to total because not all types of consumer units are shown.
Source: Calculations by New Strategist based on the Bureau of Labor Statistics 2004 Consumer Expenditure Survey

Table 55. Nonalcoholic Beverages: Market shares by household type, 2004

(percentage of total annual spending on nonalcoholic beverages accounted for by types of consumer units, 2004)

	total consumer units	total married couples	married couples, no children	married couples with children				single parent, at least one child <18	single person
				total	oldest child under 6	oldest child 6 to 17	oldest child 18 or older		
Share of total consumer units	100.0%	51.4%	22.0%	25.2%	4.8%	13.2%	7.1%	5.9%	29.0%
Share of total before-tax income	100.0	68.9	26.0	36.9	6.7	19.1	11.2	3.4	15.0
Share of total spending	100.0	65.9	25.2	35.2	6.2	18.5	10.6	4.5	17.0
NONALCOHOLIC BEVERAGES	**100.0**	**64.6**	**21.7**	**35.9**	**5.5**	**19.8**	**10.8**	**5.7**	**15.2**
Carbonated drinks, colas	100.0	63.5	22.3	34.6	4.9	18.3	11.7	5.6	15.1
Carbonated drinks, noncolas	100.0	64.5	20.4	36.3	4.3	20.0	12.4	6.3	14.5
Coffee, instant and freeze-dried	100.0	63.0	30.5	27.3	3.4	15.2	8.9	3.9	19.0
Coffee, roasted	100.0	64.0	32.1	27.2	3.8	15.0	8.6	3.5	18.2
Fruit-flavored drinks	100.0	63.6	15.1	41.4	4.5	27.3	9.6	9.0	12.3
Fruit juice, canned and bottled	100.0	62.9	20.5	35.1	6.3	19.0	9.7	6.6	16.6
Fruit juice, fresh	100.0	64.4	21.2	35.5	5.0	18.6	12.1	4.8	15.8
Fruit juice, frozen	100.0	67.1	21.4	38.5	5.3	21.5	11.9	3.3	15.2
Milk, fresh	100.0	66.4	20.3	38.8	6.4	21.5	10.9	5.9	13.8
Tea	100.0	67.4	27.9	33.2	3.6	17.0	13.2	4.5	15.1
Vegetable juice	100.0	63.4	22.0	34.1	6.7	18.1	9.3	5.6	15.7
Other nonalcoholic beverages and ice	100.0	64.3	20.5	36.8	6.2	20.9	9.6	5.2	16.3

Note: Market shares by type of consumer unit will not add to total because not all types of consumer units are shown.
Source: Calculations by New Strategist based on the Bureau of Labor Statistics 2004 Consumer Expenditure Survey

Table 56. Nonalcoholic Beverages: Average spending by race and Hispanic origin, 2004

(average annual spending of consumer units (CU) on nonalcoholic beverages, by race and Hispanic origin of consumer unit reference person, 2004)

	total consumer units	Asian	black	Hispanic	non-Hispanic white and other
Number of consumer units (in 000s)	116,282	3,957	13,773	12,298	90,424
Number of persons per CU	2.5	2.8	2.6	3.3	2.3
Average before-tax income of CU	$54,453.00	$67,705.00	$38,503.00	$43,693.00	$58,314.00
Average spending of CU, total	43,394.87	49,458.68	30,481.49	37,578.03	46,163.26
NONALCOHOLIC BEVERAGES	**509.94**	**475.78**	**415.68**	**631.93**	**508.30**
Carbonated drinks, colas	93.81	54.39	70.54	118.92	93.84
Carbonated drinks, noncolas	48.08	28.59	39.52	42.72	50.15
Coffee, instant and freeze-dried	14.64	15.08	9.06	15.88	15.43
Coffee, roasted	24.48	23.89	13.75	18.07	27.02
Fruit-flavored drinks	19.79	11.36	28.27	32.14	16.89
Fruit juice, canned and bottled	55.05	59.32	61.88	76.05	51.45
Fruit juice, fresh	22.07	28.16	22.52	26.10	21.42
Fruit juice, frozen	6.44	3.62	6.10	6.99	6.41
Milk, fresh	128.94	128.57	94.96	184.77	126.59
Tea	17.63	20.72	12.62	16.49	18.68
Vegetable juice	8.91	10.89	6.42	10.26	9.14
Other nonalcoholic beverages and ice	70.10	91.19	50.04	83.54	71.28

Note: "Asian" and "black" include Hispanics and non-Hispanics who identify themselves as being of the respective race alone. "Hispanic" includes people of any race who identify themselves as Hispanic. "Other" includes people who identify themselves as non-Hispanic and as Alaska Native, American Indian, Asian (who are also included in the "Asian" column), Native Hawaiian or other Pacific Islander, as well as non-Hispanics reporting more than one race.
Source: Bureau of Labor Statistics, unpublished tables from the 2004 Consumer Expenditure Survey

Table 57. Nonalcoholic Beverages: Indexed spending by race and Hispanic origin, 2004

(indexed average annual spending of consumer units (CU) on nonalcoholic beverages, by race and Hispanic origin of consumer unit reference person, 2004; index definition: an index of 100 is the average for all consumer units; an index of 132 means that spending by consumer units in that group is 32 percent above the average for all consumer units; an index of 68 indicates spending that is 32 percent below the average for all consumer units)

	total consumer units	Asian	black	Hispanic	non-Hispanic white and other
Average spending of CU, total	$43,395	$49,459	$30,481	$37,578	$46,163
Average spending of CU, index	100	114	70	87	106
NONALCOHOLIC BEVERAGES	100	93	82	124	100
Carbonated drinks, colas	100	58	75	127	100
Carbonated drinks, noncolas	100	59	82	89	104
Coffee, instant and freeze-dried	100	103	62	108	105
Coffee, roasted	100	98	56	74	110
Fruit-flavored drinks	100	57	143	162	85
Fruit juice, canned and bottled	100	108	112	138	93
Fruit juice, fresh	100	128	102	118	97
Fruit juice, frozen	100	56	95	109	100
Milk, fresh	100	100	74	143	98
Tea	100	118	72	94	106
Vegetable juice	100	122	72	115	103
Other nonalcoholic beverages and ice	100	130	71	119	102

Note: "Asian" and "black" include Hispanics and non-Hispanics who identify themselves as being of the respective race alone. "Hispanic" includes people of any race who identify themselves as Hispanic. "Other" includes people who identify themselves as non-Hispanic and as Alaska Native, American Indian, Asian (who are also included in the "Asian" column), Native Hawaiian or other Pacific Islander, as well as non-Hispanics reporting more than one race.
Source: Calculations by New Strategist based on the Bureau of Labor Statistics 2004 Consumer Expenditure Survey

Table 58. Nonalcoholic Beverages: Total spending by race and Hispanic origin, 2004

(total annual spending on nonalcoholic beverages, by consumer unit race and Hispanic origin groups, 2004; consumer units and dollars in thousands)

	total consumer units	Asian	black	Hispanic	non-Hispanic white and other
Number of consumer units	116,282	3,957	13,773	12,298	90,424
Total spending of all CUs	$5,046,042,273	$195,707,997	$419,821,562	$462,134,613	$4,174,266,622
NONALCOHOLIC BEVERAGES	59,296,843	1,882,661	5,725,161	7,771,475	45,962,519
Carbonated drinks, colas	10,908,414	215,221	971,547	1,462,478	8,485,388
Carbonated drinks, noncolas	5,590,839	113,131	544,309	525,371	4,534,764
Coffee, instant and freeze-dried	1,702,368	59,672	124,783	195,292	1,395,242
Coffee, roasted	2,846,583	94,533	189,379	222,225	2,443,256
Fruit-flavored drinks	2,301,221	44,952	389,363	395,258	1,527,261
Fruit juice, canned and bottled	6,401,324	234,729	852,273	935,263	4,652,315
Fruit juice, fresh	2,566,344	111,429	310,168	320,978	1,936,882
Fruit juice, frozen	748,856	14,324	84,015	85,963	579,618
Milk, fresh	14,993,401	508,751	1,307,884	2,272,301	11,446,774
Tea	2,050,052	81,989	173,815	202,794	1,689,120
Vegetable juice	1,036,073	43,092	88,423	126,177	826,475
Other nonalcoholic beverages and ice	8,151,368	360,839	689,201	1,027,375	6,445,423

Note: "Asian" and "black" include Hispanics and non-Hispanics who identify themselves as being of the respective race alone. "Hispanic" includes people of any race who identify themselves as Hispanic. "Other" includes people who identify themselves as non-Hispanic and as Alaska Native, American Indian, Asian (who are also included in the "Asian" column), Native Hawaiian or other Pacific Islander, as well as non-Hispanics reporting more than one race. Numbers may not add to total because of rounding.
Source: Calculations by New Strategist based on the Bureau of Labor Statistics 2004 Consumer Expenditure Survey

Table 59. Nonalcoholic Beverages: Market shares by race and Hispanic origin, 2004

(percentage of total annual spending on nonalcoholic beverages accounted for by consumer unit race and Hispanic origin groups, 2004)

	total consumer units	Asian	black	Hispanic	non-Hispanic white and other
Share of total consumer units	**100.0%**	**3.4%**	**11.8%**	**10.6%**	**77.8%**
Share of total before-tax income	**100.0**	**4.2**	**8.4**	**8.5**	**83.3**
Share of total spending	**100.0**	**3.9**	**8.3**	**9.2**	**82.7**
NONALCOHOLIC BEVERAGES	**100.0**	**3.2**	**9.7**	**13.1**	**77.5**
Carbonated drinks, colas	100.0	2.0	8.9	13.4	77.8
Carbonated drinks, noncolas	100.0	2.0	9.7	9.4	81.1
Coffee, instant and freeze-dried	100.0	3.5	7.3	11.5	82.0
Coffee, roasted	100.0	3.3	6.7	7.8	85.8
Fruit-flavored drinks	100.0	2.0	16.9	17.2	66.4
Fruit juice, canned and bottled	100.0	3.7	13.3	14.6	72.7
Fruit juice, fresh	100.0	4.3	12.1	12.5	75.5
Fruit juice, frozen	100.0	1.9	11.2	11.5	77.4
Milk, fresh	100.0	3.4	8.7	15.2	76.3
Tea	100.0	4.0	8.5	9.9	82.4
Vegetable juice	100.0	4.2	8.5	12.2	79.8
Other nonalcoholic beverages and ice	100.0	4.4	8.5	12.6	79.1

Note: "Asian" and "black" include Hispanics and non-Hispanics who identify themselves as being of the respective race alone. "Hispanic" includes people of any race who identify themselves as Hispanic. "Other" includes people who identify themselves as non-Hispanic and as Alaska Native, American Indian, Asian (who are also included in the "Asian" column), Native Hawaiian or other Pacific Islander, as well as non-Hispanics reporting more than one race.
Source: Calculations by New Strategist based on the Bureau of Labor Statistics 2004 Consumer Expenditure Survey

Table 60. Nonalcoholic Beverages: Average spending by region, 2004

(average annual spending of consumer units (CU) on nonalcoholic beverages, by region in which consumer unit lives, 2004)

	total consumer units	Northeast	Midwest	South	West
Number of consumer units (in 000s)	116,282	22,051	26,539	41,801	25,891
Number of persons per CU	2.5	2.4	2.4	2.5	2.6
Average before-tax income of CU	$54,453.00	$61,050.00	$53,567.00	$50,775.00	$55,682.00
Average spending of CU, total	43,394.87	46,114.89	43,370.77	39,173.65	47,921.74
NONALCOHOLIC BEVERAGES	**509.94**	**531.20**	**489.84**	**482.02**	**558.16**
Carbonated drinks, colas	93.81	80.57	99.75	95.00	97.13
Carbonated drinks, noncolas	48.08	45.58	53.44	48.35	44.22
Coffee, instant and freeze-dried	14.64	16.19	13.21	13.26	17.06
Coffee, roasted	24.48	25.80	21.93	22.60	29.06
Fruit-flavored drinks	19.79	20.17	17.05	19.81	22.30
Fruit juice, canned and bottled	55.05	67.84	50.56	49.01	58.54
Fruit juice, fresh	22.07	29.79	22.76	17.79	21.64
Fruit juice, frozen	6.44	5.56	7.66	4.08	9.77
Milk, fresh	128.94	138.31	122.53	119.37	143.16
Tea	17.63	22.81	14.60	16.56	18.07
Vegetable juice	8.91	11.72	8.81	6.55	10.42
Other nonalcoholic beverages and ice	70.10	66.86	57.54	69.64	86.79

Source: Bureau of Labor Statistics, unpublished tables from the 2004 Consumer Expenditure Survey

Table 61. Nonalcoholic Beverages: Indexed spending by region, 2004

(indexed average annual spending of consumer units (CU) on nonalcoholic beverages, by region in which consumer unit lives, 2004; index definition: an index of 100 is the average for all consumer units; an index of 132 means that spending by consumer units in that group is 32 percent above the average for all consumer units; an index of 68 indicates spending that is 32 percent below the average for all consumer units)

	total consumer units	Northeast	Midwest	South	West
Average spending of CU, total	$43,395	$46,115	$43,371	$39,174	$47,922
Average spending of CU, index	100	106	100	90	110
NONALCOHOLIC BEVERAGES	100	104	96	95	109
Carbonated drinks, colas	100	86	106	101	104
Carbonated drinks, noncolas	100	95	111	101	92
Coffee, instant and freeze-dried	100	111	90	91	117
Coffee, roasted	100	105	90	92	119
Fruit-flavored drinks	100	102	86	100	113
Fruit juice, canned and bottled	100	123	92	89	106
Fruit juice, fresh	100	135	103	81	98
Fruit juice, frozen	100	86	119	63	152
Milk, fresh	100	107	95	93	111
Tea	100	129	83	94	102
Vegetable juice	100	132	99	74	117
Other nonalcoholic beverages and ice	100	95	82	99	124

Source: Calculations by New Strategist based on the Bureau of Labor Statistics 2004 Consumer Expenditure Survey

Table 62. Nonalcoholic Beverages: Total spending by region, 2004

(total annual spending on nonalcoholic beverages, by region in which consumer unit lives, 2004; consumer units and dollars in thousands)

	total consumer units	Northeast	Midwest	South	West
Number of consumer units	116,282	22,051	26,539	41,801	25,891
Total spending of all CUs	$5,046,042,273	$1,016,879,439	$1,151,016,865	$1,637,497,744	$1,240,741,770
NONALCOHOLIC BEVERAGES	59,296,843	11,713,491	12,999,864	20,148,918	14,451,321
Carbonated drinks, colas	10,908,414	1,776,649	2,647,265	3,971,095	2,514,793
Carbonated drinks, noncolas	5,590,839	1,005,085	1,418,244	2,021,078	1,144,900
Coffee, instant and freeze-dried	1,702,368	357,006	350,580	554,281	441,700
Coffee, roasted	2,846,583	568,916	582,000	944,703	752,392
Fruit-flavored drinks	2,301,221	444,769	452,490	828,078	577,369
Fruit juice, canned and bottled	6,401,324	1,495,940	1,341,812	2,048,667	1,515,659
Fruit juice, fresh	2,566,344	656,899	604,028	743,640	560,281
Fruit juice, frozen	748,856	122,604	203,289	170,548	252,955
Milk, fresh	14,993,401	3,049,874	3,251,824	4,989,785	3,706,556
Tea	2,050,052	502,983	387,469	692,225	467,850
Vegetable juice	1,036,073	258,438	233,809	273,797	269,784
Other nonalcoholic beverages and ice	8,151,368	1,474,330	1,527,054	2,911,022	2,247,080

Note: Numbers may not add to total because of rounding.
Source: Calculations by New Strategist based on the Bureau of Labor Statistics 2004 Consumer Expenditure Survey

Table 63. Nonalcoholic Beverages: Market shares by region, 2004

(percentage of total annual spending on nonalcoholic beverages accounted for by consumer units by region, 2004)

	total consumer units	Northeast	Midwest	South	West
Share of total consumer units	100.0%	19.0%	22.8%	35.9%	22.3%
Share of total before-tax income	100.0	21.3	22.5	33.5	22.8
Share of total spending	100.0	20.2	22.8	32.5	24.6
NONALCOHOLIC BEVERAGES	**100.0**	**19.8**	**21.9**	**34.0**	**24.4**
Carbonated drinks, colas	100.0	16.3	24.3	36.4	23.1
Carbonated drinks, noncolas	100.0	18.0	25.4	36.1	20.5
Coffee, instant and freeze-dried	100.0	21.0	20.6	32.6	25.9
Coffee, roasted	100.0	20.0	20.4	33.2	26.4
Fruit-flavored drinks	100.0	19.3	19.7	36.0	25.1
Fruit juice, canned and bottled	100.0	23.4	21.0	32.0	23.7
Fruit juice, fresh	100.0	25.6	23.5	29.0	21.8
Fruit juice, frozen	100.0	16.4	27.1	22.8	33.8
Milk, fresh	100.0	20.3	21.7	33.3	24.7
Tea	100.0	24.5	18.9	33.8	22.8
Vegetable juice	100.0	24.9	22.6	26.4	26.0
Other nonalcoholic beverages and ice	100.0	18.1	18.7	35.7	27.6

Note: Numbers may not add to total because of rounding.
Source: Calculations by New Strategist based on the Bureau of Labor Statistics 2004 Consumer Expenditure Survey

Table 64. Nonalcoholic Beverages: Average spending by education, 2004

(average annual spending of consumer units (CU) on nonalcoholic beverages, by education of consumer unit reference person, 2004)

	total consumer units	less than high school graduate	high school graduate	some college	associate's degree	college graduate total	college graduate bachelor's degree	college graduate master's, professional, doctorate
Number of consumer units (in 000s)	116,282	16,829	31,005	25,317	10,678	32,452	20,684	11,768
Number of persons per CU	2.5	2.7	2.5	2.3	2.6	2.5	2.4	2.5
Average before-tax income of CU	$54,453.00	$29,094.00	$42,334.00	$46,756.00	$58,593.00	$83,825.00	$75,647.00	$98,201.00
Average spending of CU, total	43,394.87	25,421.18	35,438.55	40,877.68	48,177.36	60,712.28	56,728.41	67,801.38
NONALCOHOLIC BEVERAGES	**509.94**	**495.37**	**494.54**	**480.13**	**553.82**	**540.43**	**529.73**	**560.80**
Carbonated drinks, colas	93.81	101.43	101.63	86.48	116.23	80.80	76.99	88.07
Carbonated drinks, noncolas	48.08	43.35	50.81	47.11	52.58	47.20	45.39	50.64
Coffee, instant and freeze-dried	14.64	14.99	12.73	14.82	16.01	15.80	15.80	15.79
Coffee, roasted	24.48	18.84	21.68	23.45	31.30	28.77	27.87	30.48
Fruit-flavored drinks	19.79	22.38	18.84	22.98	18.54	17.51	18.06	16.46
Fruit juice, canned and bottled	55.05	50.43	47.90	52.05	51.27	67.64	67.10	68.67
Fruit juice, fresh	22.07	19.94	19.64	18.12	21.22	28.58	27.59	30.45
Fruit juice, frozen	6.44	6.15	5.93	5.35	8.62	7.21	7.43	6.78
Milk, fresh	128.94	141.83	125.50	115.44	136.21	133.11	131.40	136.37
Tea	17.63	13.40	16.14	17.35	20.21	20.68	20.13	21.73
Vegetable juice	8.91	7.04	8.64	8.72	7.75	10.59	11.28	9.29
Other nonalcoholic beverages and ice	70.10	55.59	65.10	68.26	73.88	82.54	80.69	86.07

Source: Bureau of Labor Statistics, unpublished tables from the 2004 Consumer Expenditure Survey

Table 65. Nonalcoholic Beverages: Indexed spending by education, 2004

(indexed average annual spending of consumer units (CU) on nonalcoholic beverages, by education of consumer unit reference person, 2004; index definition: an index of 100 is the average for all consumer units; an index of 132 means that spending by consumer units in that group is 32 percent above the average for all consumer units; an index of 68 indicates spending that is 32 percent below the average for all consumer units)

	total consumer units	less than high school graduate	high school graduate	some college	associate's degree	college graduate total	bachelor's degree	master's, professional, doctorate
Average spending of CU, total	$43,395	$25,421	$35,439	$40,878	$48,177	$60,712	$56,728	$67,801
Average spending of CU, index	100	59	82	94	111	140	131	156
NONALCOHOLIC BEVERAGES	**100**	**97**	**97**	**94**	**109**	**106**	**104**	**110**
Carbonated drinks, colas	100	108	108	92	124	86	82	94
Carbonated drinks, noncolas	100	90	106	98	109	98	94	105
Coffee, instant and freeze-dried	100	102	87	101	109	108	108	108
Coffee, roasted	100	77	89	96	128	118	114	125
Fruit-flavored drinks	100	113	95	116	94	88	91	83
Fruit juice, canned and bottled	100	92	87	95	93	123	122	125
Fruit juice, fresh	100	90	89	82	96	129	125	138
Fruit juice, frozen	100	95	92	83	134	112	115	105
Milk, fresh	100	110	97	90	106	103	102	106
Tea	100	76	92	98	115	117	114	123
Vegetable juice	100	79	97	98	87	119	127	104
Other nonalcoholic beverages and ice	100	79	93	97	105	118	115	123

Source: Calculations by New Strategist based on the Bureau of Labor Statistics 2004 Consumer Expenditure Survey

Table 66. Nonalcoholic Beverages: Total spending by education, 2004

(total annual spending on nonalcoholic beverages, by consumer unit (CU) education group, 2004; consumer units and dollars in thousands)

	total consumer units	less than high school graduate	high school graduate	some college	associate's degree	college graduate total	bachelor's degree	master's, professional, doctorate
Number of consumer units	116,282	16,829	31,005	25,317	10,678	32,452	20,684	11,768
Total spending of all CUs	$5,046,042,273	$427,813,038	$1,098,772,243	$1,034,900,225	$514,437,850	$1,970,234,911	$1,173,370,432	$797,886,640
NONALCOHOLIC BEVERAGES	**59,296,843**	**8,336,582**	**15,333,213**	**12,155,451**	**5,913,690**	**17,538,034**	**10,956,935**	**6,599,494**
Carbonated drinks, colas	10,908,414	1,706,965	3,151,038	2,189,414	561,449	2,622,122	1,592,461	1,036,408
Carbonated drinks, noncolas	5,590,839	729,537	1,575,364	1,192,684	561,449	1,531,734	938,847	595,932
Coffee, instant and freeze-dried	1,702,368	252,267	394,694	375,198	170,955	512,742	326,807	185,817
Coffee, roasted	2,846,583	317,058	672,188	593,684	334,221	933,644	576,463	358,689
Fruit-flavored drinks	2,301,221	376,633	584,134	581,785	197,970	568,235	373,553	193,701
Fruit juice, canned and bottled	6,401,324	848,686	1,485,140	1,317,750	547,461	2,195,053	1,387,896	808,109
Fruit juice, fresh	2,566,344	335,570	608,938	458,744	226,587	927,478	570,672	358,336
Fruit juice, frozen	748,856	103,498	183,860	135,446	92,044	233,979	153,682	79,787
Milk, fresh	14,993,401	2,386,857	3,891,128	2,922,594	1,454,450	4,319,686	2,717,878	1,604,802
Tea	2,050,052	225,509	500,421	439,250	215,802	671,107	416,369	255,719
Vegetable juice	1,036,073	118,476	267,883	220,764	82,755	343,667	233,316	109,325
Other nonalcoholic beverages and ice	8,151,368	935,524	2,018,426	1,728,138	788,891	2,678,588	1,668,992	1,012,872

Note: Numbers may not add to total because of rounding.
Source: Calculations by New Strategist based on the Bureau of Labor Statistics 2004 Consumer Expenditure Survey

Table 67. Nonalcoholic Beverages: Market shares by education, 2004

(percentage of total annual spending on nonalcoholic beverages accounted for by consumer unit education groups, 2004)

	total consumer units	less than high school graduate	high school graduate	some college	associate's degree	college graduate total	bachelor's degree	master's, professional, doctorate
Share of total consumer units	100.0%	14.5%	26.7%	21.8%	9.2%	27.9%	17.8%	10.1%
Share of total before-tax income	100.0	7.7	20.7	18.7	9.9	43.0	24.7	18.3
Share of total spending	100.0	8.5	21.8	20.5	10.2	39.0	23.3	15.8
NONALCOHOLIC BEVERAGES	100.0	14.1	25.9	20.5	10.0	29.6	18.5	11.1
Carbonated drinks, colas	100.0	15.6	28.9	20.1	11.4	24.0	14.6	9.5
Carbonated drinks, noncolas	100.0	13.0	28.2	21.3	10.0	30.1	16.8	10.7
Coffee, instant and freeze-dried	100.0	14.8	23.2	22.0	10.0	30.1	19.2	10.9
Coffee, roasted	100.0	11.1	23.6	20.9	11.7	32.8	20.3	12.6
Fruit-flavored drinks	100.0	16.4	25.4	25.3	8.6	24.7	16.2	8.4
Fruit juice, canned and bottled	100.0	13.3	23.2	20.6	8.6	34.3	21.7	12.6
Fruit juice, fresh	100.0	13.1	23.7	17.9	8.8	36.1	22.2	14.0
Fruit juice, frozen	100.0	13.8	24.6	18.1	12.3	31.2	20.5	10.7
Milk, fresh	100.0	15.9	26.0	19.5	9.7	28.8	18.1	10.7
Tea	100.0	11.0	24.4	21.4	10.5	32.7	20.3	12.5
Vegetable juice	100.0	11.4	25.9	21.3	8.0	33.2	22.5	10.6
Other nonalcoholic beverages and ice	100.0	11.5	24.8	21.2	9.7	32.9	20.5	12.4

Note: Numbers may not add to total because of rounding.
Source: Calculations by New Strategist based on the Bureau of Labor Statistics 2004 Consumer Expenditure Survey

Carbonated Drinks, Colas

Best customers:	Householders aged 35 to 64
	Married couples with school-aged or older children
	Hispanics
Customer trends:	Average household spending on colas may fall as boomers move out of the crowded-nest lifestage, but the younger generation's substitution of colas for coffee might limit the decline.

Cola-flavored carbonated drinks rank a lofty eighth among grocery items on which the average household spends the most. The best customers of colas are the largest households. Married couples with school-aged or older children at home spend 38 to 64 percent more than average on this item. Householders ranging in age from 35 to 64, many with children at home, spend 12 to 27 percent more than average on colas and control 66 percent of the market. Hispanics, who tend to have large families, spend 27 percent more than average on colas.

Average household spending on colas fell 2 percent between 2000 and 2004, after adjusting for inflation. Lower-priced private brands and discounters were one reasons for the decline. Average household spending on colas may continue to fall as boomers become empty-nesters and household size shrinks. But younger generations, drinking cola rather than coffee, might limit the decline.

Table 68. Carbonated drinks, colas

Total household spending	$10,908,414,420.00
Average household spends	93.81

	AVERAGE HOUSEHOLD SPENDING	BEST CUSTOMERS (index)	BIGGEST CUSTOMERS (market share)
AGE OF HOUSEHOLDER			
Average household	**$93.81**	**100**	**100.0%**
Under age 25	55.21	59	4.5
Aged 25 to 34	90.96	97	16.2
Aged 35 to 44	107.59	115	23.7
Aged 45 to 54	118.84	127	25.8
Aged 55 to 64	104.63	112	16.8
Aged 65 to 74	73.88	79	7.6
Aged 75 or older	49.98	53	5.3

	AVERAGE HOUSEHOLD SPENDING	BEST CUSTOMERS (index)	BIGGEST CUSTOMERS (market share)
HOUSEHOLD INCOME			
Average household	**$93.81**	**100**	**100.0%**
Under $20,000	64.06	68	17.0
$20,000 to $39,999	88.13	94	22.1
$40,000 to $49,999	94.73	101	9.9
$50,000 to $69,999	106.66	114	17.7
$70,000 to $79,999	105.78	113	6.3
$80,000 to $99,999	110.48	118	9.4
$100,000 or more	123.03	131	16.8
HOUSEHOLD TYPE			
Average household	**93.81**	**100**	**100.0**
Married couples	115.84	123	63.5
Married couples, no children	95.17	101	22.3
Married couples, with children	129.04	138	34.6
Oldest child under 6	96.16	103	4.9
Oldest child 6 to 17	129.91	138	18.3
Oldest child 18 or older	153.62	164	11.7
Single parent with child under 18	88.94	95	5.6
Single person	48.80	52	15.1
RACE AND HISPANIC ORIGIN			
Average household	**93.81**	**100**	**100.0**
Asian	54.39	58	2.0
Black	70.54	75	8.9
Hispanic	118.92	127	13.4
Non-Hispanic white and other	93.84	100	77.8
REGION			
Average household	**93.81**	**100**	**100.0**
Northeast	80.57	86	16.3
Midwest	99.75	106	24.3
South	95.00	101	36.4
West	97.13	104	23.1
EDUCATION			
Average household	**93.81**	**100**	**100.0**
Less than high school graduate	101.43	108	15.6
High school graduate	101.63	108	28.9
Some college	86.48	92	20.1
Associate's degree	116.23	124	11.4
College graduate	80.80	86	24.0
Bachelor's degree	76.99	82	14.6
Master's, professional, doctoral degree	88.07	94	9.5

Note: Market shares may not sum to 100.0 because of rounding and missing categories by household type. "Asian" and "black" include Hispanics and non-Hispanics who identify themselves as being of the respective race alone. "Hispanic" includes people of any race who identify themselves as Hispanic. "Other" includes people who identify themselves as non-Hispanic and as Alaska Native, American Indian, Asian (who are also included in the "Asian" row), Native Hawaiian or other Pacific Islander, as well as non-Hispanics reporting more than one race.
Source: Calculations by New Strategist based on the Bureau of Labor Statistics 2004 Consumer Expenditure Survey

Carbonated Drinks, Noncolas

Best customers: Householders aged 35 to 54

                                 Married couples with school-aged or older children

Customer trends: Average household spending on noncolas may fall as boomers move out of

                                 the crowded-nest lifestage.

The average household spends about half as much on noncola carbonated beverages as it does on colas. The best customers of noncola carbonated beverages are almost the same as the best customers of colas—the largest households. Married couples with school-aged or older children at home spend 51 to 74 percent more than the average household on this item. Householders aged 35 to 54, many with children at home, spend 21 to 27 percent more than average on noncolas and control 51 percent of the market.

Average household spending on noncola carbonated beverages fell 8 percent between 2000 and 2004, after adjusting for inflation. One factor behind the decline was price discounting by private-label manufacturers. Average household spending on noncolas may continue to fall as boomers move out of the crowded-nest lifestage.

Table 69. Carbonated drinks, noncolas

Total household spending $5,590,838,560.00
Average household spends   48.08

	AVERAGE HOUSEHOLD SPENDING	BEST CUSTOMERS (index)	BIGGEST CUSTOMERS (market share)
AGE OF HOUSEHOLDER			
Average household	**$48.08**	**100**	**100.0%**
Under age 25	34.14	71	5.4
Aged 25 to 34	44.15	92	15.4
Aged 35 to 44	57.97	121	25.0
Aged 45 to 54	61.06	127	25.9
Aged 55 to 64	50.43	105	15.8
Aged 65 to 74	35.20	73	7.1
Aged 75 or older	26.47	55	5.5

	AVERAGE HOUSEHOLD SPENDING	BEST CUSTOMERS (index)	BIGGEST CUSTOMERS (market share)
HOUSEHOLD INCOME			
Average household	**$48.08**	**100**	**100.0%**
Under $20,000	29.13	61	15.1
$20,000 to $39,999	45.66	95	22.3
$40,000 to $49,999	46.10	96	9.4
$50,000 to $69,999	54.83	114	17.7
$70,000 to $79,999	71.38	148	8.2
$80,000 to $99,999	50.29	105	8.3
$100,000 or more	67.03	139	17.9
HOUSEHOLD TYPE			
Average household	**48.08**	**100**	**100.0**
Married couples	60.32	125	64.5
Married couples, no children	44.64	93	20.4
Married couples, with children	69.39	144	36.3
Oldest child under 6	43.06	90	4.3
Oldest child 6 to 17	72.62	151	20.0
Oldest child 18 or older	83.78	174	12.4
Single parent with child under 18	51.01	106	6.3
Single person	24.10	50	14.5
RACE AND HISPANIC ORIGIN			
Average household	**48.08**	**100**	**100.0**
Asian	28.59	59	2.0
Black	39.52	82	9.7
Hispanic	42.72	89	9.4
Non-Hispanic white and other	50.15	104	81.1
REGION			
Average household	**48.08**	**100**	**100.0**
Northeast	45.58	95	18.0
Midwest	53.44	111	25.4
South	48.35	101	36.1
West	44.22	92	20.5
EDUCATION			
Average household	**48.08**	**100**	**100.0**
Less than high school graduate	43.35	90	13.0
High school graduate	50.81	106	28.2
Some college	47.11	98	21.3
Associate's degree	52.58	109	10.0
College graduate	47.20	98	27.4
Bachelor's degree	45.39	94	16.8
Master's, professional, doctoral degree	50.64	105	10.7

Note: Market shares may not sum to 100.0 because of rounding and missing categories by household type. "Asian" and "black" include Hispanics and non-Hispanics who identify themselves as being of the respective race alone. "Hispanic" includes people of any race who identify themselves as Hispanic. "Other" includes people who identify themselves as non-Hispanic and as Alaska Native, American Indian, Asian (who are also included in the "Asian" row), Native Hawaiian or other Pacific Islander, as well as non-Hispanics reporting more than one race.
Source: Calculations by New Strategist based on the Bureau of Labor Statistics 2004 Consumer Expenditure Survey

Coffee, Instant and Freeze-Dried

Best customers: Householders aged 45 to 64
                           Married couples without children at home
                           Married couples with adult children at home

Customer trends: Average household spending on instant coffee will fall as consumption declines
                           with the aging of the coffee-drinking generations.

Older householders are the biggest spenders on instant coffee. Householders aged 45 to 64 spend 11 to 47 percent more than the average household on this item and account for 47 percent of the market. Married couples without children at home (most of them empty-nesters) and those with adult children at home spend 25 to 39 percent more than average on instant coffee.

Average household spending on instant coffee fell 7 percent between 2000 and 2004, after adjusting for inflation. A decline in coffee consumption was one factor behind the drop in spending, as younger generations substitute caffeinated colas for coffee. Average household spending on instant coffee will continue to decline along with the aging of the coffee-drinking generations.

Table 70. Coffee, instant and freeze-dried

Total household spending $1,702,368,480.00
Average household spends   14.64

	AVERAGE HOUSEHOLD SPENDING	BEST CUSTOMERS (index)	BIGGEST CUSTOMERS (market share)
AGE OF HOUSEHOLDER			
Average household	**$14.64**	**100**	**100.0%**
Under age 25	4.98	34	2.6
Aged 25 to 34	10.04	69	11.5
Aged 35 to 44	14.26	97	20.2
Aged 45 to 54	21.55	147	30.0
Aged 55 to 64	16.19	111	16.6
Aged 65 to 74	14.55	99	9.6
Aged 75 or older	14.68	100	9.9

	AVERAGE HOUSEHOLD SPENDING	BEST CUSTOMERS (index)	BIGGEST CUSTOMERS (market share)
HOUSEHOLD INCOME			
Average household	**$14.64**	**100**	**100.0%**
Under $20,000	9.61	66	16.3
$20,000 to $39,999	12.33	84	19.8
$40,000 to $49,999	13.21	90	8.8
$50,000 to $69,999	15.17	104	16.1
$70,000 to $79,999	23.96	164	9.1
$80,000 to $99,999	14.69	100	8.0
$100,000 or more	23.82	163	20.9
HOUSEHOLD TYPE			
Average household	**14.64**	**100**	**100.0**
Married couples	17.93	122	63.0
Married couples, no children	20.30	139	30.5
Married couples, with children	15.90	109	27.3
Oldest child under 6	10.41	71	3.4
Oldest child 6 to 17	16.87	115	15.2
Oldest child 18 or older	18.30	125	8.9
Single parent with child under 18	9.70	66	3.9
Single person	9.60	66	19.0
RACE AND HISPANIC ORIGIN			
Average household	**14.64**	**100**	**100.0**
Asian	15.08	103	3.5
Black	9.06	62	7.3
Hispanic	15.88	108	11.5
Non-Hispanic white and other	15.43	105	82.0
REGION			
Average household	**14.64**	**100**	**100.0**
Northeast	16.19	111	21.0
Midwest	13.21	90	20.6
South	13.26	91	32.6
West	17.06	117	25.9
EDUCATION			
Average household	**14.64**	**100**	**100.0**
Less than high school graduate	14.99	102	14.8
High school graduate	12.73	87	23.2
Some college	14.82	101	22.0
Associate's degree	16.01	109	10.0
College graduate	15.80	108	30.1
Bachelor's degree	15.80	108	19.2
Master's, professional, doctoral degree	15.79	108	10.9

Note: Market shares may not sum to 100.0 because of rounding and missing categories by household type. "Asian" and "black" include Hispanics and non-Hispanics who identify themselves as being of the respective race alone. "Hispanic" includes people of any race who identify themselves as Hispanic. "Other" includes people who identify themselves as non-Hispanic and as Alaska Native, American Indian, Asian (who are also included in the "Asian" row), Native Hawaiian or other Pacific Islander, as well as non-Hispanics reporting more than one race.
Source: Calculations by New Strategist based on the Bureau of Labor Statistics 2004 Consumer Expenditure Survey

Coffee, Roasted

Best customers: Householders aged 45 to 64
Married couples without children at home
Married couples with adult children at home

Customer trends: Average household spending on roasted coffee will fall as consumption declines with the aging of the coffee-drinking generations.

Although Starbucks has been wildly successful in promoting coffee to the masses, it has not managed to stem the overall decline in coffee consumption. Younger generations increasingly get their caffeine jolt from colas rather than coffee. The biggest spenders on roasted coffee are the middle aged. Householders aged 45 to 64 spend 23 to 41 percent more than the average household on roasted coffee. Married couples without children at home (most of them empty-nesters) and those with adult children at home spend 20 to 46 percent more than average on roasted coffee and account for 41 percent of the market.

Average household spending on roasted coffee fell 19 percent between 2000 and 2004, after adjusting for inflation. Behind the decline in spending is the substitution of caffeinated colas for coffee by younger generations. Average household spending on roasted coffee will continue to decline along with the aging of the coffee-drinking generations.

Table 71. **Coffee, roasted**

| Total household spending | $2,846,583,360.00 | | |
| Average household spends | 24.48 | | |

	AVERAGE HOUSEHOLD SPENDING	BEST CUSTOMERS (index)	BIGGEST CUSTOMERS (market share)
AGE OF HOUSEHOLDER			
Average household	**$24.48**	**100**	**100.0%**
Under age 25	6.71	27	2.1
Aged 25 to 34	17.86	73	12.2
Aged 35 to 44	23.18	95	19.6
Aged 45 to 54	34.60	141	28.8
Aged 55 to 64	29.99	123	18.4
Aged 65 to 74	27.78	113	11.0
Aged 75 or older	20.22	83	8.2

	AVERAGE HOUSEHOLD SPENDING	BEST CUSTOMERS (index)	BIGGEST CUSTOMERS (market share)
HOUSEHOLD INCOME			
Average household	**$24.48**	**100**	**100.0%**
Under $20,000	14.54	59	14.8
$20,000 to $39,999	20.26	83	19.4
$40,000 to $49,999	20.24	83	8.1
$50,000 to $69,999	29.19	119	18.5
$70,000 to $79,999	35.05	143	8.0
$80,000 to $99,999	27.07	111	8.8
$100,000 or more	40.88	167	21.5
HOUSEHOLD TYPE			
Average household	**24.48**	**100**	**100.0**
Married couples	30.47	124	64.0
Married couples, no children	35.70	146	32.1
Married couples, with children	26.43	108	27.2
Oldest child under 6	19.50	80	3.8
Oldest child 6 to 17	27.70	113	15.0
Oldest child 18 or older	29.34	120	8.6
Single parent with child under 18	14.34	59	3.5
Single person	15.34	63	18.2
RACE AND HISPANIC ORIGIN			
Average household	**24.48**	**100**	**100.0**
Asian	23.89	98	3.3
Black	13.75	56	6.7
Hispanic	18.07	74	7.8
Non-Hispanic white and other	27.02	110	85.8
REGION			
Average household	**24.48**	**100**	**100.0**
Northeast	25.80	105	20.0
Midwest	21.93	90	20.4
South	22.60	92	33.2
West	29.06	119	26.4
EDUCATION			
Average household	**24.48**	**100**	**100.0**
Less than high school graduate	18.84	77	11.1
High school graduate	21.68	89	23.6
Some college	23.45	96	20.9
Associate's degree	31.30	128	11.7
College graduate	28.77	118	32.8
Bachelor's degree	27.87	114	20.3
Master's, professional, doctoral degree	30.48	125	12.6

Note: Market shares may not sum to 100.0 because of rounding and missing categories by household type. "Asian" and "black" include Hispanics and non-Hispanics who identify themselves as being of the respective race alone. "Hispanic" includes people of any race who identify themselves as Hispanic. "Other" includes people who identify themselves as non-Hispanic and as Alaska Native, American Indian, Asian (who are also included in the "Asian" row), Native Hawaiian or other Pacific Islander, as well as non-Hispanics reporting more than one race.
Source: Calculations by New Strategist based on the Bureau of Labor Statistics 2004 Consumer Expenditure Survey

Fruit-Flavored Drinks, Noncarbonated

Best customers: Householders aged 35 to 44

Married couples with school-aged children

Single parents

Blacks and Hispanics

Customer trends: Average household spending on fruit-flavored drinks may continue to decline as boomers become empty-nesters, but the decline will be limited by growing numbers of blacks and Hispanics.

The best customers of fruit-flavored drinks are younger parents with children. Married couples with school-aged children at home spend more than twice the average on this item, while single parents spend 52 percent more. Householders aged 35 to 44, most with children at home, spend 45 percent more than average on this item. Blacks spend 43 percent more than average, while Hispanics spend 62 percent more. Together, blacks and Hispanics account for more than 33 percent of spending on this item.

Average household spending on noncarbonated fruit-flavored drinks fell 7 percent between 2000 and 2004, after adjusting for inflation. The lackluster recovery following the recession of 2001 and a decline in overall grocery spending were behind the decline, as was the aging of the baby-boom generation out of the best-customer age group. Average household spending on this item may continue to decline as boomers become empty-nesters, but the decline will be limited by growing numbers of blacks and Hispanics.

Table 72. Fruit-flavored drinks, noncarbonated

Total household spending $2,301,220,780.00
Average household spends   19.79

	AVERAGE HOUSEHOLD SPENDING	BEST CUSTOMERS (index)	BIGGEST CUSTOMERS (market share)
AGE OF HOUSEHOLDER			
Average household	**$19.79**	**100**	**100.0%**
Under age 25	16.46	83	6.3
Aged 25 to 34	23.24	117	19.6
Aged 35 to 44	28.62	145	29.9
Aged 45 to 54	21.58	109	22.2
Aged 55 to 64	15.78	80	12.0
Aged 65 to 74	12.15	61	5.9
Aged 75 or older	6.93	35	3.5

	AVERAGE HOUSEHOLD SPENDING	BEST CUSTOMERS (index)	BIGGEST CUSTOMERS (market share)
HOUSEHOLD INCOME			
Average household	**$19.79**	**100**	**100.0%**
Under $20,000	13.38	68	16.8
$20,000 to $39,999	20.20	102	24.0
$40,000 to $49,999	20.00	101	9.9
$50,000 to $69,999	22.37	113	17.6
$70,000 to $79,999	26.57	134	7.5
$80,000 to $99,999	21.81	110	8.8
$100,000 or more	22.65	114	14.7
HOUSEHOLD TYPE			
Average household	**19.79**	**100**	**100.0**
Married couples	24.48	124	63.6
Married couples, no children	13.57	69	15.1
Married couples, with children	32.54	164	41.4
Oldest child under 6	18.43	93	4.5
Oldest child 6 to 17	40.81	206	27.3
Oldest child 18 or older	26.61	134	9.6
Single parent with child under 18	30.11	152	9.0
Single person	8.38	42	12.3
RACE AND HISPANIC ORIGIN			
Average household	**19.79**	**100**	**100.0**
Asian	11.36	57	2.0
Black	28.27	143	16.9
Hispanic	32.14	162	17.2
Non-Hispanic white and other	16.89	85	66.4
REGION			
Average household	**19.79**	**100**	**100.0**
Northeast	20.17	102	19.3
Midwest	17.05	86	19.7
South	19.81	100	36.0
West	22.30	113	25.1
EDUCATION			
Average household	**19.79**	**100**	**100.0**
Less than high school graduate	22.38	113	16.4
High school graduate	18.84	95	25.4
Some college	22.98	116	25.3
Associate's degree	18.54	94	8.6
College graduate	17.51	88	24.7
Bachelor's degree	18.06	91	16.2
Master's, professional, doctoral degree	16.46	83	8.4

Note: Market shares may not sum to 100.0 because of rounding and missing categories by household type. "Asian" and "black" include Hispanics and non-Hispanics who identify themselves as being of the respective race alone. "Hispanic" includes people of any race who identify themselves as Hispanic. "Other" includes people who identify themselves as non-Hispanic and as Alaska Native, American Indian, Asian (who are also included in the "Asian" row), Native Hawaiian or other Pacific Islander, as well as non-Hispanics reporting more than one race.
Source: Calculations by New Strategist based on the Bureau of Labor Statistics 2004 Consumer Expenditure Survey

Fruit Juice, Canned and Bottled

Best customers:	**Householders aged 25 to 54**
	Married couples with children at home
	Single parents
	Blacks and Hispanics
Customer trends:	**Average household spending on canned and bottled fruit juice should decline as boomers become empty-nesters, but the decline will be limited by growing numbers of blacks and Hispanics.**

Canned and bottled juice dominates fruit juice spending. Households with children are the biggest spenders on canned and bottled fruit juice. Married couples with children at home spend 39 percent more than average on this item. Single parents spend 11 percent more. Householders ranging in age from 25 to 54, most with children at home, spend 8 to 17 percent more than average on this item. Blacks spend 12 percent more, while Hispanics spend 38 percent more.

Average household spending on canned and bottled fruit juice fell 11 percent between 2000 and 2004, after adjusting for inflation. Behind the decline is the growing propensity of consumers to eat fast-food breakfasts or skip breakfast entirely. Average household spending on canned and bottled fruit juice will continue to decline as the small generation X fills the best-customer lifestage, but the decline will be limited by growing numbers of blacks and Hispanics.

Table 73. Fruit juice, canned and bottled

Total household spending	$6,401,324,100.00
Average household spends	55.05

	AVERAGE HOUSEHOLD SPENDING	BEST CUSTOMERS (index)	BIGGEST CUSTOMERS (market share)
AGE OF HOUSEHOLDER			
Average household	**$55.05**	**100**	**100.0%**
Under age 25	39.67	72	5.5
Aged 25 to 34	59.48	108	18.1
Aged 35 to 44	61.11	111	23.0
Aged 45 to 54	64.52	117	23.9
Aged 55 to 64	48.92	89	13.4
Aged 65 to 74	46.75	85	8.2
Aged 75 or older	44.15	80	8.0

	AVERAGE HOUSEHOLD SPENDING	BEST CUSTOMERS (index)	BIGGEST CUSTOMERS (market share)
HOUSEHOLD INCOME			
Average household	**$55.05**	**100**	**100.0%**
Under $20,000	36.32	66	16.4
$20,000 to $39,999	49.84	91	21.3
$40,000 to $49,999	51.37	93	9.1
$50,000 to $69,999	59.48	108	16.8
$70,000 to $79,999	69.38	126	7.0
$80,000 to $99,999	59.92	109	8.7
$100,000 or more	84.62	154	19.7
HOUSEHOLD TYPE			
Average household	**55.05**	**100**	**100.0**
Married couples	67.29	122	62.9
Married couples, no children	51.27	93	20.5
Married couples, with children	76.66	139	35.1
Oldest child under 6	72.45	132	6.3
Oldest child 6 to 17	79.06	144	19.0
Oldest child 18 or older	75.02	136	9.7
Single parent with child under 18	60.87	111	6.6
Single person	31.63	57	16.6
RACE AND HISPANIC ORIGIN			
Average household	**55.05**	**100**	**100.0**
Asian	59.32	108	3.7
Black	61.88	112	13.3
Hispanic	76.05	138	14.6
Non-Hispanic white and other	51.45	93	72.7
REGION			
Average household	**55.05**	**100**	**100.0**
Northeast	67.84	123	23.4
Midwest	50.56	92	21.0
South	49.01	89	32.0
West	58.54	106	23.7
EDUCATION			
Average household	**55.05**	**100**	**100.0**
Less than high school graduate	50.43	92	13.3
High school graduate	47.90	87	23.2
Some college	52.05	95	20.6
Associate's degree	51.27	93	8.6
College graduate	67.64	123	34.3
Bachelor's degree	67.10	122	21.7
Master's, professional, doctoral degree	68.67	125	12.6

Note: Market shares may not sum to 100.0 because of rounding and missing categories by household type. "Asian" and "black" include Hispanics and non-Hispanics who identify themselves as being of the respective race alone. "Hispanic" includes people of any race who identify themselves as Hispanic. "Other" includes people who identify themselves as non-Hispanic and as Alaska Native, American Indian, Asian (who are also included in the "Asian" row), Native Hawaiian or other Pacific Islander, as well as non-Hispanics reporting more than one race.
Source: Calculations by New Strategist based on the Bureau of Labor Statistics 2004 Consumer Expenditure Survey

Fruit Juice, Fresh

Best customers: Householders aged 35 to 64
                          Married couples with school-aged or older children
                          Asians and Hispanics

Customer trends: Average household spending on fresh fruit juice should rise as the baby-boom
                          generation moves through the 45-to-64 age group.

Middle-aged married couples are the biggest spenders on fresh fruit juice. Because fresh juice tends to be more expensive than canned or bottled juice, the best customers of fresh juice are older than the best customers of canned or bottled juice. Householders ranging in age from 35 to 64 spend 10 to 16 percent more than average on this item. Married couples with school-aged or older children at home spend 41 to 70 percent more than average on fresh fruit juice. Asians spend 28 percent more than average on this item, and Hispanics spend 18 percent more.

Average household spending on fresh fruit juice fell 14 percent between 2000 and 2004, after adjusting for inflation. Busy lifestyles were behind the spending cut, as more families eat a fast-food breakfast on the run or skip breakfast entirely. Average household spending on fresh fruit juice should increase as boomers fill the 45-to-64 age group and have more leisure time for a morning meal.

Table 74. Fruit juice, fresh

Total household spending $2,566,343,740.00
Average household spends   22.07

	AVERAGE HOUSEHOLD SPENDING	BEST CUSTOMERS (index)	BIGGEST CUSTOMERS (market share)
AGE OF HOUSEHOLDER			
Average household	**$22.07**	**100**	**100.0%**
Under age 25	9.88	45	3.4
Aged 25 to 34	23.45	106	17.8
Aged 35 to 44	24.17	110	22.7
Aged 45 to 54	25.68	116	23.7
Aged 55 to 64	25.09	114	17.1
Aged 65 to 74	19.44	88	8.5
Aged 75 or older	15.14	69	6.8

	AVERAGE HOUSEHOLD SPENDING	BEST CUSTOMERS (index)	BIGGEST CUSTOMERS (market share)
HOUSEHOLD INCOME			
Average household	**$22.07**	**100**	**100.0%**
Under $20,000	11.62	53	13.1
$20,000 to $39,999	19.03	86	20.2
$40,000 to $49,999	23.28	105	10.3
$50,000 to $69,999	22.09	100	15.6
$70,000 to $79,999	22.86	104	5.8
$80,000 to $99,999	26.91	122	9.7
$100,000 or more	40.82	185	23.8
HOUSEHOLD TYPE			
Average household	**22.07**	**100**	**100.0**
Married couples	27.64	125	64.4
Married couples, no children	21.31	97	21.2
Married couples, with children	31.09	141	35.5
Oldest child under 6	23.11	105	5.0
Oldest child 6 to 17	31.06	141	18.6
Oldest child 18 or older	37.55	170	12.1
Single parent with child under 18	18.04	82	4.8
Single person	12.03	55	15.8
RACE AND HISPANIC ORIGIN			
Average household	**22.07**	**100**	**100.0**
Asian	28.16	128	4.3
Black	22.52	102	12.1
Hispanic	26.10	118	12.5
Non-Hispanic white and other	21.42	97	75.5
REGION			
Average household	**22.07**	**100**	**100.0**
Northeast	29.79	135	25.6
Midwest	22.76	103	23.5
South	17.79	81	29.0
West	21.64	98	21.8
EDUCATION			
Average household	**22.07**	**100**	**100.0**
Less than high school graduate	19.94	90	13.1
High school graduate	19.64	89	23.7
Some college	18.12	82	17.9
Associate's degree	21.22	96	8.8
College graduate	28.58	129	36.1
Bachelor's degree	27.59	125	22.2
Master's, professional, doctoral degree	30.45	138	14.0

Note: Market shares may not sum to 100.0 because of rounding and missing categories by household type. "Asian" and "black" include Hispanics and non-Hispanics who identify themselves as being of the respective race alone. "Hispanic" includes people of any race who identify themselves as Hispanic. "Other" includes people who identify themselves as non-Hispanic and as Alaska Native, American Indian, Asian (who are also included in the "Asian" row), Native Hawaiian or other Pacific Islander, as well as non-Hispanics reporting more than one race.
Source: Calculations by New Strategist based on the Bureau of Labor Statistics 2004 Consumer Expenditure Survey

Fruit Juice, Frozen

Best customers: Married couples with school-aged or older children

Customer trends: Average household spending on frozen fruit juice will continue to decline as growing numbers of customers choose fruit juice that requires no preparation.

The largest households are the best customers of frozen fruit juice. Married couples with school-aged or older children at home spend 62 to 67 percent more than the average household on this item.

Average household spending on frozen fruit juice fell by an enormous 45 percent between 2000 and 2004, after adjusting for inflation. This decline occurred because consumers are looking for more convenience in serving fruit juice, and because they are eating breakfast out more often or skipping it entirely. Average household spending on frozen fruit juice is likely to continue to decline as more customers choose fruit juice that requires no preparation.

Table 75. Fruit juice, frozen

Total household spending $748,856,080.00
Average household spends   6.44

	AVERAGE HOUSEHOLD SPENDING	BEST CUSTOMERS (index)	BIGGEST CUSTOMERS (market share)
AGE OF HOUSEHOLDER			
Average household	**$6.44**	**100**	**100.0%**
Under age 25	4.64	72	5.5
Aged 25 to 34	5.78	90	15.0
Aged 35 to 44	7.42	115	23.8
Aged 45 to 54	6.49	101	20.6
Aged 55 to 64	5.66	88	13.2
Aged 65 to 74	5.65	88	8.5
Aged 75 or older	8.90	138	13.7

	AVERAGE HOUSEHOLD SPENDING	BEST CUSTOMERS (index)	BIGGEST CUSTOMERS (market share)
HOUSEHOLD INCOME			
Average household	**$6.44**	**100**	**100.0%**
Under $20,000	4.86	75	18.8
$20,000 to $39,999	5.70	89	20.8
$40,000 to $49,999	6.20	96	9.4
$50,000 to $69,999	7.70	120	18.6
$70,000 to $79,999	7.02	109	6.1
$80,000 to $99,999	8.40	130	10.4
$100,000 or more	7.65	119	15.3
HOUSEHOLD TYPE			
Average household	**6.44**	**100**	**100.0**
Married couples	8.40	130	67.1
Married couples, no children	6.27	97	21.4
Married couples, with children	9.84	153	38.5
Oldest child under 6	7.09	110	5.3
Oldest child 6 to 17	10.46	162	21.5
Oldest child 18 or older	10.73	167	11.9
Single parent with child under 18	3.59	56	3.3
Single person	3.38	52	15.2
RACE AND HISPANIC ORIGIN			
Average household	**6.44**	**100**	**100.0**
Asian	3.62	56	1.9
Black	6.10	95	11.2
Hispanic	6.99	109	11.5
Non-Hispanic white and other	6.41	100	77.4
REGION			
Average household	**6.44**	**100**	**100.0**
Northeast	5.56	86	16.4
Midwest	7.66	119	27.1
South	4.08	63	22.8
West	9.77	152	33.8
EDUCATION			
Average household	**6.44**	**100**	**100.0**
Less than high school graduate	6.15	95	13.8
High school graduate	5.93	92	24.6
Some college	5.35	83	18.1
Associate's degree	8.62	134	12.3
College graduate	7.21	112	31.2
Bachelor's degree	7.43	115	20.5
Master's, professional, doctoral degree	6.78	105	10.7

Note: Market shares may not sum to 100.0 because of rounding and missing categories by household type. "Asian" and "black" include Hispanics and non-Hispanics who identify themselves as being of the respective race alone. "Hispanic" includes people of any race who identify themselves as Hispanic. "Other" includes people who identify themselves as non-Hispanic and as Alaska Native, American Indian, Asian (who are also included in the "Asian" row), Native Hawaiian or other Pacific Islander, as well as non-Hispanics reporting more than one race.
Source: Calculations by New Strategist based on the Bureau of Labor Statistics 2004 Consumer Expenditure Survey

Milk, Fresh

Best customers: Householders aged 35 to 44
Married couples with children at home
Hispanics

Customer trends: Average household spending on milk will fall as boomers become
empty-nesters.

The best customers of milk are households with children. Married couples with children at home spend 54 percent more than the average household on this item. Householders aged 35 to 44, most with children, spend 23 percent more than average on milk. Hispanics, who tend to have large households, spend 43 percent more than average on this item.

Average household spending on milk fell 2 percent between 2000 and 2004, after adjusting for inflation. Behind the decline is the exiting of the baby-boom generation out of the best-customer lifestage. Another factor is the substitution of sodas, juices, and other drinks for milk. Average household spending on milk will continue to decline as boomers become empty-nesters.

Table 76. Milk, fresh

Total household spending $14,993,401,080.00
Average household spends   128.94

	AVERAGE HOUSEHOLD SPENDING	BEST CUSTOMERS (index)	BIGGEST CUSTOMERS (market share)
AGE OF HOUSEHOLDER			
Average household	**$128.94**	**100**	**100.0%**
Under age 25	79.18	61	4.7
Aged 25 to 34	132.79	103	17.2
Aged 35 to 44	159.16	123	25.6
Aged 45 to 54	143.87	112	22.8
Aged 55 to 64	120.21	93	14.0
Aged 65 to 74	109.30	85	8.2
Aged 75 or older	97.47	76	7.5

	AVERAGE HOUSEHOLD SPENDING	BEST CUSTOMERS (index)	BIGGEST CUSTOMERS (market share)
HOUSEHOLD INCOME			
Average household	**$128.94**	**100**	**100.0%**
Under $20,000	93.50	73	18.0
$20,000 to $39,999	120.79	94	22.0
$40,000 to $49,999	128.65	100	9.8
$50,000 to $69,999	136.51	106	16.5
$70,000 to $79,999	138.50	107	6.0
$80,000 to $99,999	147.07	114	9.1
$100,000 or more	179.41	139	17.9
HOUSEHOLD TYPE			
Average household	**128.94**	**100**	**100.0**
Married couples	166.56	129	66.4
Married couples, no children	118.67	92	20.3
Married couples, with children	198.70	154	38.8
Oldest child under 6	171.98	133	6.4
Oldest child 6 to 17	210.08	163	21.5
Oldest child 18 or older	196.41	152	10.9
Single parent with child under 18	128.33	100	5.9
Single person	61.43	48	13.8
RACE AND HISPANIC ORIGIN			
Average household	**128.94**	**100**	**100.0**
Asian	128.57	100	3.4
Black	94.96	74	8.7
Hispanic	184.77	143	15.2
Non-Hispanic white and other	126.59	98	76.3
REGION			
Average household	**128.94**	**100**	**100.0**
Northeast	138.31	107	20.3
Midwest	122.53	95	21.7
South	119.37	93	33.3
West	143.16	111	24.7
EDUCATION			
Average household	**128.94**	**100**	**100.0**
Less than high school graduate	141.83	110	15.9
High school graduate	125.50	97	26.0
Some college	115.44	90	19.5
Associate's degree	136.21	106	9.7
College graduate	133.11	103	28.8
Bachelor's degree	131.40	102	18.1
Master's, professional, doctoral degree	136.37	106	10.7

Note: Market shares may not sum to 100.0 because of rounding and missing categories by household type. "Asian" and "black" include Hispanics and non-Hispanics who identify themselves as being of the respective race alone. "Hispanic" includes people of any race who identify themselves as Hispanic. "Other" includes people who identify themselves as non-Hispanic and as Alaska Native, American Indian, Asian (who are also included in the "Asian" row), Native Hawaiian or other Pacific Islander, as well as non-Hispanics reporting more than one race.
Source: Calculations by New Strategist based on the Bureau of Labor Statistics 2004 Consumer Expenditure Survey

Other Nonalcoholic Beverages and Ice
(excludes carbonated drinks, coffee, fruit and vegetable juices, fruit-flavored drinks, and tea)

Best customers: Householders aged 35 to 54
                           Married couples with children at home
                           Asians and Hispanics

Customer trends: Average household spending on this item may stabilize as boomers exit the
                           best-customer lifestage.

Americans spend a considerable sum on "other nonalcoholic beverages," a category that includes bottled water and sports drinks—an average of $70.10 in 2004. The best customers of other nonalcoholic beverages are the largest households. Married couples with children at home spend 46 percent more than the average household on this item. Householders aged 35 to 54, many with children at home, spend 24 to 28 percent more than average on other nonalcoholic beverages. Asians spend 30 percent more than the average, and Hispanics, who tend to have large households, spend 19 percent more.

Average household spending on other nonalcoholic beverages and ice rose by an enormous 68 percent between 2000 and 2004, after adjusting for inflation. Behind the spending increase was the growing popularity of bottled water and sports drinks. Average household spending on this item may stabilize as boomers exit the best-customer lifestage.

Table 77. Other nonalcoholic beverages and ice
(excludes carbonated drinks, coffee, fruit and vegetable juices, fruit-flavored drinks, and tea)

Total household spending $8,151,368,200.00
Average household spends   70.10

	AVERAGE HOUSEHOLD SPENDING	BEST CUSTOMERS (index)	BIGGEST CUSTOMERS (market share)
AGE OF HOUSEHOLDER			
Average household	**$70.10**	**100**	**100.0%**
Under age 25	39.99	57	4.3
Aged 25 to 34	79.32	113	18.9
Aged 35 to 44	89.43	128	26.4
Aged 45 to 54	86.61	124	25.2
Aged 55 to 64	57.78	82	12.4
Aged 65 to 74	46.49	66	6.4
Aged 75 or older	43.42	62	6.1

	AVERAGE HOUSEHOLD SPENDING	BEST CUSTOMERS (index)	BIGGEST CUSTOMERS (market share)
HOUSEHOLD INCOME			
Average household	**$70.10**	**100**	**100.0%**
Under $20,000	39.26	56	13.9
$20,000 to $39,999	49.36	70	16.5
$40,000 to $49,999	65.76	94	9.2
$50,000 to $69,999	81.96	117	18.2
$70,000 to $79,999	89.88	128	7.1
$80,000 to $99,999	89.17	127	10.1
$100,000 or more	129.74	185	23.8
HOUSEHOLD TYPE			
Average household	**70.10**	**100**	**100.0**
Married couples	87.66	125	64.3
Married couples, no children	65.31	93	20.5
Married couples, with children	102.37	146	36.8
Oldest child under 6	90.84	130	6.2
Oldest child 6 to 17	110.62	158	20.9
Oldest child 18 or older	94.41	135	9.6
Single parent with child under 18	61.74	88	5.2
Single person	39.53	56	16.3
RACE AND HISPANIC ORIGIN			
Average household	**70.10**	**100**	**100.0**
Asian	91.19	130	4.4
Black	50.04	71	8.5
Hispanic	83.54	119	12.6
Non-Hispanic white and other	71.28	102	79.1
REGION			
Average household	**70.10**	**100**	**100.0**
Northeast	66.86	95	18.1
Midwest	57.54	82	18.7
South	69.64	99	35.7
West	86.79	124	27.6
EDUCATION			
Average household	**70.10**	**100**	**100.0**
Less than high school graduate	55.59	79	11.5
High school graduate	65.10	93	24.8
Some college	68.26	97	21.2
Associate's degree	73.88	105	9.7
College graduate	82.54	118	32.9
Bachelor's degree	80.69	115	20.5
Master's, professional, doctoral degree	86.07	123	12.4

Note: Market shares may not sum to 100.0 because of rounding and missing categories by household type. "Asian" and "black" include Hispanics and non-Hispanics who identify themselves as being of the respective race alone. "Hispanic" includes people of any race who identify themselves as Hispanic. "Other" includes people who identify themselves as non-Hispanic and as Alaska Native, American Indian, Asian (who are also included in the "Asian" row), Native Hawaiian or other Pacific Islander, as well as non-Hispanics reporting more than one race.
Source: Calculations by New Strategist based on the Bureau of Labor Statistics 2004 Consumer Expenditure Survey

Tea

Although tea has been getting good press, with nutritionists touting its health benefits, Americans spend far less on tea than on coffee. In 2004, the average household spent just 45 percent as much on tea ($17.63) as on roasted and instant coffee ($39.12). Older householders are the best customers of tea. Householders aged 35 to 64 spend 8 to 32 percent more than average on this item. Married couples without children at home (most of them empty-nesters) spend 27 percent more than average on tea. Couples with school-aged or older children at home (the largest households) spend 29 to 85 percent more than average this item. Asians spend 18 percent more than the average on tea, and households in the Northeast spend 29 percent more.

Average household spending on tea rose a modest 2 percent between 2000 and 2004, after adjusting for inflation. Behind the small rise is the preference of younger generations for carbonated drinks over coffee or tea. Average household spending on tea may rise, however, as boomers fill the best-customer age group.

Table 78. Tea

| Total household spending | $2,050,051,660.00 |
| Average household spends | 17.63 |

	AVERAGE HOUSEHOLD SPENDING	BEST CUSTOMERS (index)	BIGGEST CUSTOMERS (market share)
AGE OF HOUSEHOLDER			
Average household	**$17.63**	**100**	**100.0%**
Under age 25	13.24	75	5.7
Aged 25 to 34	14.75	84	14.0
Aged 35 to 44	18.96	108	22.3
Aged 45 to 54	23.28	132	26.9
Aged 55 to 64	19.36	110	16.5
Aged 65 to 74	14.91	85	8.2
Aged 75 or older	11.54	65	6.5

	AVERAGE HOUSEHOLD SPENDING	BEST CUSTOMERS (index)	BIGGEST CUSTOMERS (market share)
HOUSEHOLD INCOME			
Average household	**$17.63**	**100**	**100.0%**
Under $20,000	10.84	61	15.3
$20,000 to $39,999	12.58	71	16.8
$40,000 to $49,999	16.75	95	9.3
$50,000 to $69,999	22.61	128	19.9
$70,000 to $79,999	18.73	106	5.9
$80,000 to $99,999	18.79	107	8.5
$100,000 or more	32.26	183	23.5
HOUSEHOLD TYPE			
Average household	**17.63**	**100**	**100.0**
Married couples	23.10	131	67.4
Married couples, no children	22.37	127	27.9
Married couples, with children	23.25	132	33.2
Oldest child under 6	13.01	74	3.6
Oldest child 6 to 17	22.72	129	17.0
Oldest child 18 or older	32.60	185	13.2
Single parent with child under 18	13.43	76	4.5
Single person	9.16	52	15.1
RACE AND HISPANIC ORIGIN			
Average household	**17.63**	**100**	**100.0**
Asian	20.72	118	4.0
Black	12.62	72	8.5
Hispanic	16.49	94	9.9
Non-Hispanic white and other	18.68	106	82.4
REGION			
Average household	**17.63**	**100**	**100.0**
Northeast	22.81	129	24.5
Midwest	14.60	83	18.9
South	16.56	94	33.8
West	18.07	102	22.8
EDUCATION			
Average household	**17.63**	**100**	**100.0**
Less than high school graduate	13.40	76	11.0
High school graduate	16.14	92	24.4
Some college	17.35	98	21.4
Associate's degree	20.21	115	10.5
College graduate	20.68	117	32.7
Bachelor's degree	20.13	114	20.3
Master's, professional, doctoral degree	21.73	123	12.5

Note: Market shares may not sum to 100.0 because of rounding and missing categories by household type. "Asian" and "black" include Hispanics and non-Hispanics who identify themselves as being of the respective race alone. "Hispanic" includes people of any race who identify themselves as Hispanic. "Other" includes people who identify themselves as non-Hispanic and as Alaska Native, American Indian, Asian (who are also included in the "Asian" row), Native Hawaiian or other Pacific Islander, as well as non-Hispanics reporting more than one race.
Source: Calculations by New Strategist based on the Bureau of Labor Statistics 2004 Consumer Expenditure Survey

Vegetable Juice, Fresh and Canned

Best customers:	Married couples with children at home Asians and Hispanics
Customer trends:	Average household spending on vegetable juice may continue to fall as younger generations, preferring sodas, fill the best-customer lifestage.

The biggest spenders on vegetable juice are the largest households. Married couples with children at home spend 36 percent more than average on this item. Asians spend 22 percent more than average on vegetable juices and Hispanics spend 15 percent more.

Average household spending on vegetable juice fell 15 percent between 2000 and 2004, after adjusting for inflation. Behind the decline is the preference of boomers and younger generations for carbonated drinks and fruit juice over vegetable juice. Average household spending on vegetable juice could continue to decline as younger generations fill the best-customer lifestage.

Table 79. Vegetable juice, fresh and canned

Total household spending	$1,036,072,620.00
Average household spends	8.91

	AVERAGE HOUSEHOLD SPENDING	BEST CUSTOMERS (index)	BIGGEST CUSTOMERS (market share)
AGE OF HOUSEHOLDER			
Average household	**$8.91**	**100**	**100.0%**
Under age 25	4.83	54	4.1
Aged 25 to 34	7.93	89	14.9
Aged 35 to 44	10.31	116	24.0
Aged 45 to 54	10.49	118	24.0
Aged 55 to 64	7.92	89	13.4
Aged 65 to 74	10.48	118	11.4
Aged 75 or older	7.42	83	8.3

	AVERAGE HOUSEHOLD SPENDING	BEST CUSTOMERS (index)	BIGGEST CUSTOMERS (market share)
HOUSEHOLD INCOME			
Average household	**$8.91**	**100**	**100.0%**
Under $20,000	5.67	64	15.8
$20,000 to $39,999	8.16	92	21.5
$40,000 to $49,999	6.41	72	7.0
$50,000 to $69,999	9.23	104	16.1
$70,000 to $79,999	11.52	129	7.2
$80,000 to $99,999	10.13	114	9.0
$100,000 or more	15.46	174	22.3
HOUSEHOLD TYPE			
Average household	**8.91**	**100**	**100.0**
Married couples	10.99	123	63.4
Married couples, no children	8.90	100	22.0
Married couples, with children	12.08	136	34.1
Oldest child under 6	12.42	139	6.7
Oldest child 6 to 17	12.20	137	18.1
Oldest child 18 or older	11.55	130	9.3
Single parent with child under 18	8.47	95	5.6
Single person	4.82	54	15.7
RACE AND HISPANIC ORIGIN			
Average household	**8.91**	**100**	**100.0**
Asian	10.89	122	4.2
Black	6.42	72	8.5
Hispanic	10.26	115	12.2
Non-Hispanic white and other	9.14	103	79.8
REGION			
Average household	**8.91**	**100**	**100.0**
Northeast	11.72	132	24.9
Midwest	8.81	99	22.6
South	6.55	74	26.4
West	10.42	117	26.0
EDUCATION			
Average household	**8.91**	**100**	**100.0**
Less than high school graduate	7.04	79	11.4
High school graduate	8.64	97	25.9
Some college	8.72	98	21.3
Associate's degree	7.75	87	8.0
College graduate	10.59	119	33.2
Bachelor's degree	11.28	127	22.5
Master's, professional, doctoral degree	9.29	104	10.6

Note: Market shares may not sum to 100.0 because of rounding and missing categories by household type. "Asian" and "black" include Hispanics and non-Hispanics who identify themselves as being of the respective race alone. "Hispanic" includes people of any race who identify themselves as Hispanic. "Other" includes people who identify themselves as non-Hispanic and as Alaska Native, American Indian, Asian (who are also included in the "Asian" row), Native Hawaiian or other Pacific Islander, as well as non-Hispanics reporting more than one race.
Source: Calculations by New Strategist based on the Bureau of Labor Statistics 2004 Consumer Expenditure Survey

Appendix: Spending by Product and Service Ranked by Amount Spent, 2004

(average annual spending of consumer units on products and services, ranked by amount spent, 2004)

Deductions for Social Security	$3,432.61
Vehicle purchases (net outlay)	3,397.07
Groceries (also shown by individual category)	3,346.82
Mortgage interest	2,785.37
Restaurants (also shown by meal category)	2,259.72
Rent	2,125.93
Gasoline and motor oil	1,597.56
Federal income taxes	1,518.95
Property taxes	1,391.17
Health insurance	1,331.71
Electricity	1,064.41
Vehicle insurance	964.37
Restaurant dinners	795.59
Restaurant lunches	725.07
Vehicle maintenance and repairs	651.66
Women's clothes	631.01
Residential phone service	592.31
Cash contributions to church, religious organizations	565.11
College tuition	541.35
Maintenance and repair services, owned homes	530.63
Deductions for private pensions	518.59
Cable TV or community antenna	471.01
Alcoholic beverages (beer and wine also shown separately)	459.27
Natural gas	424.02
Nonpayroll deposit to retirement plans	400.54
State and local income taxes	397.82
Life and other personal insurance	390.34
Cellular phone service	378.39
Prescription drugs	349.41
Vehicle finance charges	323.41
Men's clothes	317.28
Homeowner's insurance	314.75
Cash gifts to nonhousehold members	302.93
Restaurant snacks	297.45
Lodging on trips	277.89
Airline fares	275.94
Beef	265.34
Personal care services	264.09
Cigarettes	264.05
Water and sewerage maintenance	242.54
Dental services	240.60
Motorized recreational vehicles	229.60
Leased vehicles	216.58
Restaurant breakfasts	210.06
Beer	207.63
Day care centers, nurseries, and preschools	193.51
Fresh fruits	186.74
Fresh vegetables	182.94
Pork	181.14
Child support	165.10
Finance charges other than mortgage and vehicle	158.18
Decorative items for the home	158.10
Cash contributions to charities	157.51
Poultry	155.61

Women's footwear	$153.81
Interest paid, home equity loan/line of credit	150.62
Laundry and cleaning supplies	148.56
Cosmetics, perfume, bath preparations	147.41
Physician's services	146.58
Taxes except federal, state, local, personal property, and property	146.39
Elementary and high school tuition	142.80
Carbonated drinks	141.89
Movie, theater, opera, and ballet tickets	140.49
Computer information services (Internet)	139.46
Owned vacation homes	137.22
Computers and computer hardware, nonbusiness use	134.57
Fresh milk	128.94
Fish and seafood	127.80
Legal fees	127.50
School expenses (except tuition, books, supplies)	119.39
Wine	116.84
Jewelry	113.72
Cheese	113.67
Men's footwear	110.67
Pet food	110.31
Girls' (2 to 15) clothes	107.60
Prepared food except frozen, salads, and desserts	102.74
Fees for participant sports	100.70
Toys, games, arts and crafts, and tricycles	99.21
Social, recreation, civic club membership	98.19
Gardening, lawn care service	95.08
Sofas	94.74
Television sets	92.75
Expenses for other properties	91.63
Boys' (2 to 15) clothes	88.88
Housekeeping services	88.85
Ready-to-eat and cooked cereals	86.69
Potato chips and other snacks	86.06
Cleansing and toilet tissue, paper towels and napkins	85.84
Bedroom linens	85.72
Lawn and garden supplies	83.44
Candy and chewing gum	83.13
Trash and garbage collection	82.77
Support for college students	82.49
Fees for recreational lessons	82.42
Bedroom furniture except mattresses and springs	81.32
Vehicle registration, state	80.92
Nonprescription drugs	80.31
Infants' (under age 2) clothes	78.51
Deductions for government retirement	78.45
Veterinary services	78.38
Frozen prepared foods, except meals	78.11
Stationery, stationery supplies, giftwrap	74.86
Postage	74.12
Home maintenance and repair materials, owned homes	73.33
Lunch meats (cold cuts)	72.99
Nonalcoholic beverages (except carbonated, coffee, fruit-flavored drinks, and tea) and ice	70.10
Lotteries and gambling losses	66.54
Funeral expenses	65.78
Wall units, cabinets, and other occasional furniture	65.05
Fuel oil	64.19
Hair care products	63.90
School lunches	63.39
Babysitting and child care	63.21
Ice cream products	60.22

Professional laundry and dry cleaning	$60.18
School books, supplies, equipment for college	58.86
Catered affairs	58.56
Pet purchase, supplies, medicine	57.85
Housing while attending school	57.73
Unmotored recreational vehicles	55.39
Books, except for school	55.19
Canned and bottled fruit juice	55.05
Mattresses and springs	53.56
Athletic gear, game tables, and exercise equipment	53.07
Bread other than white	52.59
Ship fares	52.10
Admission to sporting events	52.06
Refrigerators, freezers	51.27
Accounting fees	51.22
Hospital services other than room	51.20
Nonprescription vitamins	50.57
Lawn and garden equipment	48.79
Eyeglasses and contact lenses	47.56
Alimony	47.29
Cookies	46.57
Intracity mass transit fares	46.32
Cash contributions to educational institutions	46.06
Bottled gas	45.20
Occupational expenses	43.10
Video cassettes, tapes, and discs	42.63
Biscuits and rolls	42.11
Eggs	41.84
Newspaper subscriptions	41.76
Living room chairs	41.65
Indoor plants, fresh flowers	41.52
Care in convalescent or nursing home	41.33
Kitchen and dining room furniture	41.26
Sauces and gravies	40.94
Groceries on trips	40.86
Ground rent	40.10
Hospital room	40.01
Medical services by professionals other than physician	39.54
Coffee	39.12
Cakes and cupcakes	39.04
Eyecare services	38.89
Alcoholic beverages purchased on trips	38.37
Rented vehicles	38.27
Canned and packaged soups	36.50
Rent as pay	36.08
Outdoor equipment	35.99
Boys' footwear	35.92
Rental of video cassettes, tapes, films, and discs	35.61
CDs, audio tapes, records	35.26
White bread	35.04
Care for elderly, invalids, handicapped	34.96
Coin-operated apparel laundry and dry cleaning	34.86
Oral hygiene products	34.63
Canned vegetables	34.49
Deodorants, feminine hygiene, miscellaneous personal care	34.33
Moving, storage, freight express	33.91
Power tools	33.44
Photographic equipment and supplies (except film)	33.16
Film and film processing	32.49
Cooking stoves, ovens	32.42
Hunting and fishing equipment	31.82
Frozen meals	31.79
Topicals and dressings	31.53
Personal property taxes	31.17

Nuts	$31.01
Washing machines	30.65
Baby food	30.08
Parking fees	29.41
Taxi fares and limousine services	29.05
Fats and oils	28.56
Property management, owned home	28.55
Frozen vegetables	28.50
Girls' footwear	28.34
Wall-to-wall carpeting	27.98
Food or board at school	27.89
Electric floor-cleaning equipment	27.71
Salad dressings	27.44
School tuition (except college, elementary, high school)	27.13
Maintenance and repair services, rented home	26.94
Telephones and accessories	26.83
Lab tests, X-rays	26.75
Pasta, cornmeal, and other cereal products	26.55
Frozen and refrigerated bakery products	26.32
Prepared salads	25.43
Pet services	25.07
Gift of stocks, bonds, and mutual funds to nonhousehold members	24.97
Crackers	24.60
Meals as pay	24.45
VCRs and video disc players	24.05
Floor coverings, nonpermanent	24.00
Sweetrolls, coffee cakes, doughnuts	23.59
Window coverings	23.47
Sound equipment	23.39
Frankfurters	22.52
Salt, spices, other seasonings	22.22
Tableware, nonelectric kitchenware	22.20
Fresh fruit juice	22.07
Tobacco products except cigarettes	22.07
Jams, preserves, other sweets	22.04
Clothes dryers	22.03
Butter	21.81
Watches	21.51
Bathroom linens	21.26
Glassware	20.88
Musical instruments and accessories	20.06
Baking needs	19.97
Noncarbonated fruit-flavored drinks	19.79
Tolls	19.23
Curtains and draperies	19.22
Computer software and accessories for nonbusiness use	19.06
Shaving needs	18.71
Checking accounts, other bank service charges	18.70
Phone cards	18.51
Rice	18.46
Video game hardware and software	18.34
Nonelectric cookware	18.10
Intercity train fares	17.84
Closet and storage items	17.83
Tea	17.63
Small electric kitchen appliances	17.27
Cash contributions to political organizations	16.58
Lamps and lighting fixtures	16.40
Photographer fees	16.23
Canned fruits	16.19
Outdoor furniture	16.18
Sugar	16.10
Laundry and cleaning equipment	15.72
Home security system service fee	15.57

Cream	$15.39
Hearing aids	15.21
Magazine subscriptions	14.88
Living room tables	14.77
Appliance repair, including service center	14.53
Dishwashers (built-in), garbage disposals, range hoods	14.34
Pies, tarts, turnovers	13.99
Prepared flour mixes	13.78
School books, supplies, equipment for elementary, high school	13.56
Camping equipment	13.48
Cemetery lots, vaults, maintenance fees	13.48
China and other dinnerware	13.47
Automobile service clubs	13.12
Material for making clothes	13.05
Peanut butter	12.52
Lamb, organ meats	12.48
Services for termite/pest control	12.04
Office furniture for home use	11.37
Bicycles	11.34
Sewing materials for household items (except clothes)	11.20
Prepared desserts	10.91
Nondairy cream and imitation milk	10.80
Wood	10.61
Olives, pickles, relishes	10.52
Local transportation on trips	10.00
Kitchen and dining room linens	9.84
Electric personal care appliances	9.74
Tape recorders and players	9.71
Dried vegetables	9.58
Margarine	9.57
Newspapers, nonsubscriptions	9.44
Intercity bus fares	9.35
Vehicle inspection	9.29
Slipcovers, decorative pillows	9.12
Vegetable juice	9.06
Infants' furniture	8.44
Microwave ovens	8.43
Magazines, nonsubscriptions	8.36
Flour	8.32
Adult day care centers	8.03
Infants' equipment	7.86
Sewing patterns and notions	7.82
Clocks	7.64
Reupholstering, furniture repair	7.35
Repairs/rentals of household equipment	7.29
Driver's license	7.16
Supportive and convalescent medical equipment	7.16
Tenant's insurance	7.06
Vehicle registration, local	6.90
Artificial sweeteners	6.85
Medical equipment for general use	6.75
Luggage	6.63
Delivery services	6.52
Frozen fruit juice	6.44
Hair accessories	6.37
Management and upkeep for security, owned home	6.36
Dried fruit	6.35
Hand tools	6.11
Shopping club membership fees	5.72
Docking and landing fees	5.62
Alteration, repair and tailoring of apparel and accessories	5.12
Towing charges	5.08
Maintenance and repair materials, rented home	5.07
Portable heating and cooling equipment	4.83

Water sports equipment	$4.65
Window air conditioners	4.36
Winter sports equipment	4.17
Compact disc, tape, record, and video mail order clubs	4.15
Repair of computer systems for nonbusiness use	4.03
Flatware	4.02
Watch and jewelry repair	3.82
Fireworks	3.75
Rental of supportive, convalescent medical equipment	3.74
Coin-operated household laundry and dry cleaning (nonclothing)	3.71
Radios	3.67
Sewing machines	3.59
Frozen fruits	3.53
Parking at owned home	3.43
Playground equipment	3.33
Bread and cracker products	3.25
Safe deposit box rental	3.22
Water softening service	3.06
Repair of TV, radio, and sound equipment	3.02
Deductions for railroad retirement	2.67
Rental and repair of sports equipment	2.49
Credit card memberships	2.41
School books, supplies, equipment for day care, nursery, other	2.32
Clothing rental	2.28
Rental and repair of musical instruments	2.28
Rental of furniture	2.22
Septic tank cleaning	2.16
Visual goods	2.10
Smoking accessories	2.02
Wigs and hairpieces	1.90
Rental of medical equipment	1.88
Plastic dinnerware	1.82
Appliance rental	1.75
Termite/pest control products	1.53
Pinball, electronic video games	1.51
Calculators	1.44
Portable dishwasher	1.22
Shoe repair and other shoe service	1.12
Smoke alarms	1.03
Pager service	1.01
Repair and rental of photographic equipment	0.99
Professional laundry and dry cleaning, sent out (nonclothing)	0.94
Business equipment for home use	0.94
Rental of television ets	0.81
Satellite dishes	0.77
School bus	0.74
…Telephone answering devices	0.62
Repair of miscellaneous household equipment and furnishings	0.54
Clothing storage	0.47
Silver serving pieces	0.30
Rental of VCR, radio, and sound equipment	0.11

Source: Calculations by New Strategist based on the 2004 Consumer Expenditure Survey

Glossary

age The age of the reference person.

average spending The average amount spent per household. The Bureau of Labor Statistics calculates the average for all households in a segment, not just for those who purchased an item. For items purchased by most households—such as bread—average spending figures are an accurate account of actual spending. For products and services purchased by few households during a year's time—such as cars—the average amount spent is much less than what purchasers spend. See Table 1 for the percentage of consumer units reporting an expenditure and the average amount spent by purchasers.

baby boom Generation born from 1946 through 1964.

baby bust Generation born from 1965 through 1976. Also known as generation X.

consumer unit Defined as follows:

• All members of a household who are related by blood, marriage, adoption, or other legal arrangements.

• A person living alone or sharing a household with others or living as a roomer in a private home or lodging house or in permanent living quarters in a hotel or motel, but who is financially independent.

• Two or more persons living together who pool their income to make joint expenditure decisions. Financial independence is determined by the three major expense categories: housing, food, and other living expenses. To be considered financially independent, at least two of the three major expense categories have to be provided by the respondent. For convenience, called household in the text of this book.

consumer unit, composition of The classification of interview households by type according to (1) relationship of other household members to the reference person; (2) age of the children to the reference person; and (3) combination of relationship to the reference person and age of the children. Stepchildren and adopted children are included with the reference person's own children.

education of reference person The number of years of formal education of the reference person based on the highest grade completed. If the respondent was enrolled at the time of interview, the grade being attended is the one recorded. Those not reporting their education are classified under no school or not reported.

expenditure The transaction cost including excise and sales taxes of goods and services acquired during the survey period. The full cost of each purchase is recorded even though full payment may not have been made at the date of purchase. Expenditure estimates include gifts. Excluded from expenditures are purchases or portions of purchases directly assignable to business purposes and periodic credit or installment payments on goods and services already acquired.

generation X Generation born from 1965 through 1976. Also known as the baby bust.

Hispanic origin The self-identified Hispanic origin of the consumer unit reference person. All consumer units are included in one of two Hispanic origin groups based on the reference person's Hispanic origin: Hispanic or non-Hispanic. Hispanics may be of any race.

household According to the Census Bureau, all the people who occupy a household. A group of unrelated people who share a housing unit as roommates or unmarried partners is also counted as a household. Households do not include group quarters such as college dormitories, prisons, or nursing homes. A household may contain more than one consumer unit. The terms "household" and "consumer unit" are used interchangeably in this book.

income before taxes The total money earnings and selected money receipts accruing to a consumer unit during the 12 months prior to the interview date. Income includes the following components:

• *wages and salaries* Includes total money earnings for all members of the consumer unit aged 14 or older from all jobs, including civilian wages and salaries, Armed Forces pay and allowances, piece-rate payments, commissions, tips, National Guard or Reserve pay (received for training periods), and cash bonuses before deductions for taxes, pensions, union dues, etc.

• *self-employment income* Includes net business and farm income, which consists of net income (gross receipts minus operating expenses) from a profession or unincorporated business or from the operation of a farm by an owner, tenant, or sharecropper. If the business or farm is a partnership, only an appropriate share of net income is recorded. Losses are also recorded.

• *Social Security, private and government retirement* Includes payments by the federal government made under retirement, survivor, and disability insurance programs to retired persons, dependents of deceased insured workers, or to disabled workers; and private pensions or retirement benefits received by retired persons or their survivors, either directly or through an insurance company.

• *interest, dividends, rental income, and other property income* Includes interest income on savings or bonds; payments made by a corporation to its stockholders, periodic receipts from estates or trust funds; net income or loss from the rental of property, real estate, or farms, and net income or loss from roomers or boarders.

• *unemployment and workers' compensation and veterans' benefits* Includes income from unemployment compensation and workers' compensation, and veterans' payments including educational benefits, but excluding military retirement.

• *public assistance, supplemental security income, and food stamps* Includes public assistance or welfare, including that received from job training grants; supplemental security income paid by federal, state, and local welfare agencies to low-income persons who are aged 65 or older, blind, or disabled; and the value of food stamps obtained.

• *regular contributions for support* Includes alimony and child support as well as any regular contributions from persons outside the consumer unit.

• *other income* Includes money income from care of foster children, cash scholarships, fellowships, or stipends not based on working; and meals and rent as pay.

indexed spending Indexed spending figures compare the spending of particular demographic segments with that of the average household. To compute an index, the amount spent on an item by a demographic segment is divided by the amount spent on the item by the average household. That figure is then multiplied by 100. An index of 100 is the average for all households. An index of 132 means average spending by households in a segment is 32 percent above average (100 plus 32). An index of 75 means average spending by households in a segment is 25 percent below average (100 minus 25). Indexed spending figures identify the consumer units that spend the most on a product or service.

market share The market share is the percentage of total household spending on an item that is accounted for by a demographic segment. Market shares are calculated by dividing a demographic segment's total spending on an item by the total spending of all households on the item. Total spending on an item for all households is calculated by multiplying average spending by the total number of households. Total spending on an item for a demographic segment is calculated by multiplying the segment's average spending by the number of households in the segment. Market shares reveal the demographic segments that account for the largest share of spending on a product or service.

millennials Generation born from 1977 through 1994.

race The self-identified race of the consumer unit reference person. All consumer units are included in one of three racial groups: Asian, black, or "white and other." "Other" includes Alaska Natives, American Indians, Native Hawaiians, other Pacific Islanders, and persons reporting more than one race. Hispanics may be of any race.

reference person The first member mentioned by the respondent when asked to "Start with the name of the person or one of the persons who owns or rents the home." It is with respect to this person that the relationship of other consumer unit members is determined. Also called the householder or head of household.

region Consumer units are classified according to their address at the time of their participation in the survey. The four major census regions of the United States are the following state groupings:

• *Northeast:* Connecticut, Maine, Massachusetts, New Hampshire, New Jersey, New York, Pennsylvania, Rhode Island, and Vermont.

• *Midwest:* Illinois, Indiana, Iowa, Kansas, Michigan, Minnesota, Missouri, Nebraska, North Dakota, Ohio, South Dakota, and Wisconsin.

• *South:* Alabama, Arkansas, Delaware, District of Columbia, Georgia, Kentucky, Louisiana, Maryland, Mississippi, North Carolina, Oklahoma, South Carolina, Tennessee, Texas, Virginia, and West Virginia.

• *West:* Alaska, Arizona, California, Colorado, Hawaii, Idaho, Montana, Nevada, New Mexico, Oregon, Utah, Washington, and Wyoming.

Date Due

APR 1 1 2007			